THROUGH THEIR EYES

BEYOND THE PAGE

Edited By Donna Samworth

First published in Great Britain in 2020 by:

Young Writers
Remus House
Coltsfoot Drive
Peterborough
PE2 9BF
Telephone: 01733 890066
Website: www.youngwriters.co.uk

All Rights Reserved
Book Design by Ashley Janson
© Copyright Contributors 2020
Softback ISBN 978-1-80015-012-6

Printed and bound in the UK by BookPrintingUK
Website: www.bookprintinguk.com
YB0446EX

FOREWORD

Since 1991, here at Young Writers we have celebrated the awesome power of creative writing, especially in young adults, where it can serve as a vital method of expressing strong (and sometimes difficult) emotions, a conduit to develop empathy, and a safe, non-judgemental place to explore one's own place in the world. With every poem we see the effort and thought that each pupil published in this book has put into their work and by creating this anthology we hope to encourage them further with the ultimate goal of sparking a life-long love of writing.

Through Their Eyes challenged young writers to open their minds and pen bold, powerful poems from the points-of-view of any person or concept they could imagine – from celebrities and politicians to animals and inanimate objects, or even just to give us a glimpse of the world as they experience it. The result is this fierce collection of poetry that by turns questions injustice, imagines the innermost thoughts of influential figures or simply has fun.

The nature of the topic means that contentious or controversial figures may have been chosen as the narrators, and as such some poems may contain views or thoughts that, although may represent those of the person being written about, by no means reflect the opinions or feelings of either the author or us here at Young Writers.

We encourage young writers to express themselves and address subjects that matter to them, which sometimes means writing about sensitive or difficult topics. If you have been affected by any issues raised in this book, details on where to find help can be found at *www.youngwriters.co.uk/info/other/contact-lines*

CONTENTS

Independent Entries

Mia Sayers (13)	1
Tayyibah Latif (15)	2
Sophia Sills (13)	9
Brooke Luckock (15)	10
Nusrat Begum (17)	14
Lily Harbron (17)	17
Yasmeen Mia (10)	18
Debbie Afolayan	22
Tara Sapkota (16)	25
Esther Ojo Eboiyehi (17)	26
Amrah Janoofar (16)	28
Tanish Kirodian (11)	30
Arwen Carr (16)	34
Jasmeen Banya (15)	36
Arani Ganeshwaran (14)	38
Vedanta Warad (12)	40
Neha Narne (12)	44
Pollyanna Morris (12)	47
Callum Dickson (13)	48
Thomas Lynn-Gilbert	50
Lola White	53
Jessica Travers-Spencer (12)	54
Dhriti Thakkar (15)	56
Satiya Bekelcha Bekelcha Yaya	58
Hannah Lynch	60
Bethany Painter (12)	62
Jamie See	64
Zara Eila Calvin (13)	66
Mia Rock (13)	68
Tushita Gupta	70
Faye-Marie Dyke (17)	72
Grace Jenman (17)	74
Millie Webb (13)	76
Paige Jasper (17)	78
Jonathan Nkenge (12)	80
Manasvi Kommuri (13)	82
Lily Johnson (13)	84
Evelyn Thomas	86
Lily Hills (12)	88
Kairi Savage (11)	90
Adam Atkins (12)	92
Jessica Williamson (13)	94
Rayan Bhuiyan	96
Althea Beliran (16)	98
Ruth Sloper (12)	100
Alfie Reece Conal Wilson (13)	102
Evelyn Edwards (12)	104
Libby Pearse (13)	106
Abi Bartlett	108
Joelle Delta Williams (15)	110
Sanah Sygle (12)	112
Jasmine Balind-Ayoola (16)	114
Esther Higgins Mcvey (14)	116
Britney Limbaya Basuama (15)	118
Dhruv Maheshwari	120
Hiba Mohamed Efhil (15)	122
Noah Robinson (16)	124
Zainab Soogun	126
Noor Haque Prieto (12)	128
Tanisha Kaur (13)	130
Eric Shaw (12)	132
Amy Jane Clewes (12)	134
Amelie Hunter (12)	136
Sophie Edwards (12)	138
Sofija Latinkic (11)	139
Isabelle Main	140
Amber Igbo (15)	141
Ben Winchcombe (12)	142
Isabel Hall (17)	144

Name	Page
Taaliyah Parris-Sarrington (16)	146
Dylan Ridley (12)	148
Aimee Grace Heaney-McKee (15)	149
Rosabella Rajack (16)	150
Leah-Rose Manning (14)	151
Maisy-Ilar Moazzenkivi	152
Zaeem Karnachi (11)	154
Jessica Douglas (12)	155
Megan Frost (18)	156
George Ludlow (18)	157
Sakeena Rajpal (17)	158
Chloe Dark (16)	159
Ele Pike (14)	160
Melody Wright (13)	162
Megan Powell (12)	163
Robert James Tibulca (11)	164
Sherise Amanda Hudlin (11)	165
Maya Bazarnicka (11)	166
Cerys Rawlinson (15)	167
Alfie Williams (13)	168
Prabhas Vedagiri (16)	170
Tegan Markey (12)	171
Wiktoria Maszorek	172
Sophie Mulvenna (13)	173
Mia Patton (14)	174
Amelia McEleavey (15)	175
Ewan Collier (12)	176
Athviga Saththiyanthiran (12)	177
Bailey Evatt (17)	178
Iman Mahmood (13)	180
Prachi Patel (14)	181
Faith Gebre (13)	182
Brooke Peto (11)	183
Sabrina Mohammad (14)	184
Bruk Alemshet (12)	186
Daniel Laws	187
Axel Bas Davies	188
Juliet Gyan (15)	189
Brandon Ellis (13)	190
Alexander Rate (13)	191
Ruqaya Bint Aslam (11)	192
Natalie Stocker	193
Amber McIntosh	194
Scarlet Barras (17)	195
Max Lavin (12)	196
Lily Healey (13)	197
Kayla Vicente (17)	198
Erika Lang (16)	199
Max Alner (13)	200
Laith Bixby (12)	201
Jayden Bianchina (12)	202
Kayleigh (15)	203
Farah Khalif (17)	204
Grayce Kimberley (15)	205
Talia Martin (13)	206
Aaron Speak	207
Ruqqiya Shahid	208
Yusuf (11)	209
Jo-Andrea Mirembe (18)	210
Hawwaa' Bint Mahmood (16)	212
Jessica Hughes	213
Anastasia Bobosco (13)	214
Tara Olawoye (16)	215
Eliza Khaliq (11)	216
Gabriella Smith (13)	217
Shanice Steele-Henry (11)	218
Varnan Saththiyanthiran (14)	219
Brooke Gander (13)	220
Libby Laredo (11)	221
Shania Miah	222
Imogen Reynolds (13)	223
Joshua Lyon	224
Riley Lake (12)	225
Lola Swan (13)	226
Grace Winterton (14)	227
Bruno Correia	228
Ahmed Muhammad (11)	229
Neive Sarah Homewood (11)	230
Eva Doherty	231
Lois Ashfield (13)	232
Maeva-Grace Arzur-Kean (13)	233
Ifesinachi Chinwuko (12)	234
Lauren Carter (15)	235
Nicholas Bors-Sterian (12)	236
Abbie Hooper	237
Mofijinfoluwa Olayiwola (11)	238

Honey Parkhouse	239
Kiara Campos Ribeiro	240
Ahad Usman (13)	241
Tricia Currie	242
Oliver Coburn (13)	243
Lilian Turner (16)	244
Milla Shuttleworth (13)	245
Bronwyn Greenaway (11)	246
Melanie Safe (17)	247
Henry Burns (12)	248
Will Keeley	249
Katie McCabe (15)	250
Aragan Sureskumar (14)	251
Isla Ennis-Smillie	252

THE POEMS

A German Void

Peril, relentless, menacing,
I manipulate and trap these people in my empty words and promises until the point that I crush them from their freedom,
Human, I am not, I'm just a decrepit, corrupt man who must endure ever antagonising second of his polluted thoughts,
Everyone sees my flaws, sees my face, hears my words,
But do they really see me?
Do they see the ache of my meagre heart?
Or my preternatural and disorientated mind?
I'm suffocating, I'm being swallowed whole by the horrors that flood my void-like mind,
When I look in a mirror, I no longer see me, all I see is a man who feeds off the torture and agony of others.
They shout 'monster', they spit at my feet, then they die by my heartless hand,
"Be a leader," they said. "Help this dying, pathetic excuse for a country and make it better again"
If only I knew what my mind would do to itself,
If I only knew how it would trap me with my shameful thoughts and desires,
"Be a leader," they said. "Don't show mercy, don't be loved, be feared"
I thought this would make me whole,
But in the end,
I'm just a German void.

Mia Sayers (13)

Lockdown 2020

A mysterious scent has arrived
Spreading its wings over the world
People in desperation are confined
To a spiritual starvation
Or a mental or physical illness
Which have thousands of witnesses
Being pulled through the same sensations
Because there are no motions.

Your life's work has swerved off the track,
Don't fear! There is another lane,
Intricated with different rules
To keep you sane
With no moral blame.

Staggering through a tunnel of suffocation,
Missing the feeling of elation,
Freedom and all the rest
Our rights are deeply distressed.

Reassurance and sense
Is being drawn;
For how long?

Innocent eyes are locked to the screen,
Not at all sensitive,
Forget themselves on it,
Not recognising who is getting hit?

Capturing their attention
Throughout the day
No real exercise -
It carries on into the night.

Us robots are helpless,
We have no real insight
To a Divine Supplication.

Wasting our lives on a remote
Which controls our senses
Isn't there another way
To keep ourselves growing,
Building and expanding our horizon?

Our tools, intellect, skills are long forgotten,
Your licence has been dissolved
As only minute details have been resolved.

Cloaks have been adorned in
One-arrowed fashion,
Our nation has crumbled,
Under the weight of ungratefulness
Such powers do we have -
Not enough for you and me
Are withering at two ends.

Where is our say?
My hunger of values is not there
As it gave me a scare.

Running to the stores,
In army-sized groups,
Throttling any minor in our way
Pushing with a powerful anxiety,
It affects our society.

Punching a grey feather
And losing our tempers
Not looking at others who don't have enough,
Is a sign of selfishness -
Come on! We've got to stock; six months straight.

What defences do we have?
Our armour is penetrable
Except for those who know
The True Reality.

Great Britain is not the same
As it plays her own game.
Double-edged, surviving at all lengths
It has its own sense.

With Her Majesty's blessings upon us,
"We will win at all costs"
With a dramatic fuss!

Like a bird gliding above,
Free, with no great burden
It doesn't need to acquire a surgeon.

Year 2020 has brought
Sharp tastes to our mouths,
A warning - a test echoed
Through these trials.

We must work together
To achieve our goals -
Who cares if so and so
Gets the credit?
I am no politician.

Money, wealth and fame
Are delivered at our doorsteps
No entry needed
As everything is sandwiched.

These three things make us happy,
They are just, worldly objects -
Temporary - unbalanced.

We live for them
But they will not come
With us - when we leave.
For does it not say
'Death is inevitable'?

How will you carry It
Into the earth?
It will be left behind;
You will be forgotten.

And we will carry on
Until we are forgotten.
What next?

Flowery lines are strung over,
Musking the true lining,
Disguising and wrapping up
Devastating numbers.

So the song has a new lyric,
Things aren't going our way.
Why is that?

In addition to...

"Wake up sleepers from this slumber!"
Open your eyes to the true reality,
Wake up! Look around,
You shall be astound
If you are not blind
To the essence of Spirituality.

Our beliefs have fooled us,
Into this one-dimensional chamber,
We shut ourselves from this
And feel the painful hollowness.

Excuses are being linked to a chain,
No one listens to us,
A question we ask,
Remains unanswered,

As they do not want to look pathetic
In the eyes of society.

It is easy to say 'excuses'
Hard to say "I don't know"
For that is the truth.

Reputation matters in all times,
Simply because it is sublime.

Wake up! This is a taste of a bitter medicine -
The wise ones find the sweetness and warnings in this.
Falling down on their knees,
They seek forgiveness,
Repenting, begging to be saved -

Have you thought of the sudden calamities?
Deception is being painted by us everywhere.
These appearances came without a warning.

Signs of the Hour have approached,
We have been warned
In the Qur'an - the only true -
Pure wholesome book on Earth as well as the Hadiths.

What have I prepared for this?
Will my money, wealth, fame,
Be of any assistance?

The question lies in front of us,
We make no move to it

Simply because the wool is pulled over eyes -
We are drowning in lies!

This disturbs me greatly.
Our society is no longer in unity,
Each stanza has been sanctioned,
So that you may build a mansion.

What am I preparing for my,
Account/ judgement/ record/ story
And my extravagant explanation?

Tayyibah Latif (15)

Auschwitz

The pungent smell of fear wafted into my nose,
The sighing, the crying, the dying grows,
All louder by the minute, yet nothing can be heard,
This was Auschwitz, the theatre of the absurd.

I was greeted to this terrible experience by bodies scattered on the floor,
I made an oath to myself, that would not be me at the end of the war,
The first night was the worst, I could not sleep, though I was deprived,
All that mattered was my life, so far, I had survived.

My work was gruesome, awful and horrifically cruel,
I picked the clothes from the dead, the gassed, bathed in a blood pool,
Eleven long hours stretched, day by day, week by week,
Yet I still had the desire to survive, though it was meek.

My mother, my father and my sister, my brother,
All dead, all gassed, one after another,
A burning flame of great vengeance flared inside me,
I had to survive this deathtrap, oh please, hear my plea.

Hatred and murder; a sickening reality,
A lost generation, over 6 million deaths, yet not me,
Why did this happen? Why did they hate us? Where is their self-control?
They took away the lives of millions, all that is left is a girl without a soul.

Sophia Sills (13)

Umbrella

Leaves crunch under foot.
I feel a soft breeze against my face.
My dog's eyes scanning for danger,
And helping me walk ahead.

Others are relied on to keep me safe,
I never stray too far from home.
It was me who pleaded for my parents to let me walk alone,
Now I wish they said "No"

There's always a risk.
A fear of walking into something;
The accident my dog losing focus would cause,
Maybe someone will decide I'm a good target,
And that is scarier than anything else.

They could be male or female.
They could have an array of intentions:
From greed and entitlement,
To cruelty and pure evil.

Then:
They watch their target for a while,
Access how easy it'll be,
They could take thirty minutes,
Or they could take thirty seconds,
Then they act.

It's a risk for everyone,
But I can't see it coming.

I feel the first few droplets of rain on my hair,
I start to walk quicker to try and avoid a storm.
My dog hesitates,
She gives a low, quiet growl,
Which she often does if there's a potential danger.
She starts walking again,
Much faster.
I hear a voice try to hush her,
My stomach drops,
The rain starts falling harder.

My dog is pulling me to walk faster, she doesn't have to,
I'm soaking wet, scared to the brink of tears
I hear the voice talking to me, matching my quickening pace
The wind starts blowing.

I try to tell him to go away, but my voice gets caught in my throat.
My dog is walking between us, on my left.
The voice is saying things that should not be said;
Saying nice things, but in the wrong way, and for the wrong reasons.
I feel the water on my cheeks,
Unsure sure if it's from the harsh wind and rain,
Or my tears finally breaking out.

I hear a quick movement, an angry movement.
He makes an annoying comment about me being rude for not responding,
His hand tries to take a firm grip on my shoulder.
I try to run, but I trip.
My dog stands between us, trying her best to protect me.
There's a rumble of thunder in the sky.

I then hear a woman yell my name
She runs up to me.
She helps me up.
Asks me if I'm okay.
It's my mother.
I grab my dog's harness.
My mother shares her umbrella.
She tells me the man ran away.
She said I was safe now,
I believed her,
Because I knew I was.
The rain was still falling, but I couldn't feel it under the umbrella.
There are higher risks for people like me,
And I'll always have someone with an umbrella.
But sadly,
Not everyone will.

What could've happened to me-
If mum didn't show up?
What if my dog didn't protect me?

Who were they? What were their intentions?
Why me?

We'll never truly know the answers
But we can assume that they aren't good.
We can never know if he was evil,
Or if it was just a bad decision made in the moment.
What can be known:
That he isn't the first
And he won't be the last person,
To make that decision,
And make someone who couldn't possibly fight back, scared for their lives.

My dog hesitates,
She gives a low, quiet growl,
Which she often does if there's potential danger.
She starts walking again.

Brooke Luckock (15)

I Want To Be Happy

As the night arrives quicker and the days become shorter,
winter dawns upon us.
The frosty air nips at my nose,
I stare at the lifelessness of day and I can't help but feel a bit fussed.
I pull my coat closer to my body, sighing loudly;
the days are nothing but dreary and cold.
As I stare at the looming grey sky,
I acknowledge the sunshine has lost its glimmer of gold.
I frown slightly, as my thoughts begin to head towards the lack of emotion I feel,
I realise how my chest often feels more heavy.
I twiddle and play with my thumbs,
shivering due to the cold air enveloping me;
life just feels more messy.
The clouds begin to grow darker, a warning to the people of Britain-
I sigh - the rain falls often.
Although sorrow and solemn washes over me,
the rain earns my bittersweet relief and causes my heart to soften.

My depression has engulfed me as the daily rays of light are nowhere to be seen.
I anticipate for the sweet songbirds' chirps and the honeybees' buzz;
I am quite keen.

I am aware there will be better days to come,
perhaps not now, and perhaps not in months or years,
but for now, it seems that I will always remain glum.
I wish I could be happy just like those who surround me,
to God, I hope She hears my pleas.
I wait and wait, trying to remain optimistic until spring comes around,
It's so close, but thoughts of winter and death always make my heart heavy and earn a frown.

I try my best to live a happy life alongside my depression,
but as I grow older, the only way to make myself feel an inch of joy is suppression.
I draw, I write, I sing and I bake,
but as I do so, my hands always seem to lose grip and shake.
Tears find their ways rolling down my face, another depressive episode,
I just need my space.
I push and push people away, they just want to help me or so they say.
They don't understand that I'm drowning on my own,
yet I know I can't blame them because people cannot help what is not shown.
Perhaps I'll always have my depression at my side,
it's a burden that I carry yet I chose to continue my stride.

In South Asian cultures, mental health issues are demonized and laughed at, it's not an issue which I can discuss with my parents in our daily chats.

Perhaps when mental health is not the butt of all jokes in South Asian cultures,
where all Asian aunties hoard around you
and ask questions about your mental state like flock of savage vultures
I will be able to talk to a professional and get the help I deserve,
but for now I will keep quiet and reserved.
To be quiet and to be submissive are the essential qualities of a good Asian girl,
those enforced characteristics make me want to hurl.

I am living human being with emotions and feelings,
and yes, I have depression too, and I usually do feel very blue.

Yet I know there are better days to come,
and I will be happy once more,
and so will those who struggle silently alongside me, I am very sure.
So hang in there, person who reads this,
there will be a time where mental health is not dismissed and on that day,
I just want to say
that I am proud of you for coming so far,
I hope and pray your world is no longer grey.

Nusrat Begum (17)

Pandemic

Stay home they say, wash hands and do not go outside
No friends to see, no school to visit, only in the garden to plain hide
Food shops with limited numbers, queues going out the door
Quick! Shove on that mask whilst Grandad stays home, safe and snores

Colouring books, reading, at home workouts in the dozen
I miss my nan, my family and best of all my cousins
We try our best to make the most and ensure we are alright
But by the time I see my friends they would have grown a foot in height

BBQs, Netflix, Spotify - doesn't seem half bad
Only a shame we are stuck in all day, losing our wits and going half-mad
Every day we lace our trainers and pace the roads we know
If we see some people, we cross the road and keep our heads down low

What a sad day today may seem,
Sometimes I feel like a hare, caught in full beam

But just remember the stay at home tick bomb is getting less and less
And remind yourself why we are doing this - to protect our NHS
In a few years time, all this chaos will be safe in the past
Britain, we need to push through now, to ensure we finish this thing fast.

Lily Harbron (17)

The Poem Of It

The darkness that follows,
Leading her on,
It comes with a shadow that can never be gone,
It creeps up quickly,
Too fast to be seen,
Sometimes it can even be as small as a bean,
Twisting and turning,
It stalks her as prey,
Just so it can suddenly leap and temptingly say,
That it isn't a lion so fierce and so proud,
Nor the magnificent tiger who can stand his ground,
Not the rhino who can heave and hump,
But it, who can see all through a jump,
It, who claims the gift of all-knowing,
It, who says it is life and death,
It, who claims the cause of snowing,
It, who says it is the cause of theft,
It says it is God,
As thin as rod,
But we know that's not true,
Who is what and what is who,
It comes to say boo,
But it really isn't good,
Don't mess with It,
But if you really should,

Dig a large pit,
And hope it falls into it,
It's very unwise to trifle with it,
It knows all plans and all plans know it,
Trees are on its side,
It's a long ride,
She found it disapproving,
It would not stop moving,
It was hissing like a snake,
Poking her with a rake,
It stole it from a garden,
It was heading towards Barden,
To disrupt a peaceful town,
Villagers it let down,
It pierced their ears with high-pitched shrieks,
It was the worst sound they'd heard over the weeks,
It jumped into the hay,
Let us all pray,
There was a lifetime more supply of hay,
It ripped the hay apart,
And burnt it in a fire,
That wasn't the worst part,
Stakes are getting higher,
It tore the crops from the ground,
Setting each one ablaze,
On the villagers it downed,
It must've disturbed the sheeps' graze,

They all packed their bags,
Taking all the clean rags,
Gathering the food,
Apples that weren't rotten,
Two of each animal they owned,
It was quite crude,
Taking all their best cotton,
They were okay that It was alone,
It pointed and teased,
It pointed and laughed,
Lands they could've leased,
Statues they could've carved,
The villagers sighed and left their hometown,
Each one of them drooping with a miserable frown,
It was not okay,
It didn't play,
It grabbed a villager unnoticed,
Plans the villagers could've practised,
It was not an easy opponent,
It killed its component,
It is a beast formed from magic,
Blood of every animal, body of a man,
Such a scene was very tragic,
It will never mind what it can,
It stabbed the girl,
And left no traces,
It did it with a swirl,

The villagers it faces,
It shouts it killed the girl,
Her parents come running,
They sob, they hurl,
The brother comes running,
It is quite pleased that it destroyed Barden,
The villagers planned to curse it with a burden,
But they forgot the plans,
It knows all plans and all plans know it,
It killed them on the spot before the cursing,
So if you bump into it,
Remember to think,
It knows all plans and all plans know it,
It is evil,
Very brief,
The monster comes out of him at night,
And that ferocious monster will fight,
It is not God,
But it is strong,
It is wrong,
And remember,
It is it.

Yasmeen Mia (10)

Australian Bush Fires - Through Their Eyes

Another ordinary day is what we think until we're
Taken by surprise;
An unwelcoming knock on the door,
A frightened, panicked man, face lined with fear,
"Get out! It isn't safe!"

Taken by surprise,
His terrified expression soon matches our own.
A frightened, panicked man, face lined with fear
Soon turns our lives into something we cannot bear.

His terrified expression soon matches our own.
Clambering to safety, we witness the flames
Turn our lives into something we cannot bear
Tree roots trip us up as we run.

Clambering to safety, we witness the
Flames' spark and crackle, hiss and snap.
Tree roots trip us up as we run.
Our home burns before our eyes

Flames spark and crackle, hiss and snap
As though they are animals. They devour
Our home, it burns before our eyes,
As we run to safety. But is safety not our home?

As though they are animals, they devour
The trees to which we depend on for oxygen.
We run to safety, but is safety not our home?
Our home is no longer our refuge, the fire has made this clear

The trees to which we depend on for oxygen -
They cry out for help, but all in vain.
Our home is no longer our refuge, the fire has made this clear
Its vicious embers set light to our pathway

We cry out for help, but all in vain,
The fire grows stronger while we grow weaker.
Its vicious embers set light to our pathway;
There's nowhere to go. We're trapped.

The fire grows stronger while we grow weaker
It devours Australia, hungry and fierce.
'There's nowhere to go. We're trapped,'
Is what I think as I reach for my father's hand

It devours Australia, hungry and fierce
My whole life could be burnt away in an instant
Is what I think, as I reach for my father's hand
Thick smoke envelopes the air around me.

My whole life could be burnt away in an instant.
Fire is hot, fire is a murderer

Thick smoke envelopes the air around me
Fills my nostrils, pollutes my oxygen.

Fire is hot, fire is a murderer
But fire has forgotten that although it
Fills my nostrils, pollutes my oxygen
Fire is fire, and hope is hope.

Fire has forgotten that although it
Kills and destroys the land
Although it licks up bush fires with its almighty tongue
Although it steals my oxygen, and my home
Fire is fire, and there is hope
For Australia.

Debbie Afolayan

At The Front Line

The enemy bears no knife from which wounds can heal
Instead it impinges the worst burdens to feel:
Fevers, coughs, stealing breath from a lung.
War isn't a crescendo that gunfire's sung.
War is the rising alarm before a flatline,
A whining monitor screeching a heart's decline.

Wake up, unsure of what the day will bring,
Nothing to shield us from the suffering.
At home you watch the figures soar,
At work we see, first-hand, the deadly war.
Walking straight into danger to provide aid,
Nothing braver than the courage we displayed.

The retired, the students, they called on us all,
Sacrificing to save the nation - prevent its fall.
Unprecedented, they would repeatedly say.
Still, head-on went the doctors every day.
Living away to protect those that we love,
Relying on our gear - the mask, the glove.

See, war washed ashore in the form of a disease,
A ruthless monster that took lives with ease,
Fight or flight? Yet we chose to endure
Battling on, praying for a cure.
Bravery unmatched, forever in the debt
Of the heroes who persisted, lest we forget.

Tara Sapkota (16)

The War To End All War

Over centuries there has been bloodshed over another,
could this silent killer be the end of it all? I wondered
I want to naively believe that this profound immorality and wickedness that slowly crept into our society,
disconcerting our once peaceful life could be the end of it all.
I often wonder, *could this be a punishment*
for those who are now innocently dead?
I asked myself, *could it have been prevented or was it really unavoidable?*
Could it really be their time to go to the heavens?
This feels so wrong, people losing their loved ones over the invincible enemy.
Now is not the time for who is superior, it's the time for togetherness if we are to win against this unending war.
This deadly virus slowly moves in the air, attacking the most vulnerable in the most aggressive way,
slowly taking their precious lives;
Clearly this dangerous killer has no boundaries,
slowly moving, awaiting it next victim,
world leaders are not exempted against this enemy.
It's the time for us to save lives and stay indoors,
it's the time to contribute to the effort of our heroes who are putting themselves out there,
and it's time to pay tributes to the once future generations who have now lost their right of growing old.
For the future generation,

I've great concern if this silent killer doesn't put an end to this war and bring togetherness within the globe.
I don't know what will, do you?
It may seem like a long road to the end of this unending fight
but with your help of staying at home,
we will make a road to peaceful better days.
Surely behind ever darkness we will see the light in our lives again
the joy of family, togetherness, hope, happiness and community
shall surely be a thing of the present.
By faith, and with faith alone, we shall embrace the immortal love of humanity;
Within our heart we are soaring through the portal,
To eternal light.
Time changes it all yet it's only moving forward,
it will be behind us this dim shadow we all face,
in this time of fear.
With the abundance of togetherness and our love for humanity,
we shall fight your vile ambush.

Esther Ojo Eboiyehi (17)

Superpower

Everyone walks past...
Not even bothering to spare a glance,
Let alone give us at least one chance.
Invisible is what we are to their eyes,
They presume we are just a big lie.
To them we are just a rotten plague to the human race,
When they see us they begin to quicken their pace.
They look at us with distaste on their faces,
Hoping that one day we will erase,
They assume we chose this path.
But how can they assume when they haven't lived a day like us?
Not all of us had a choice
But to even say that, none of us have a voice...

They walk past us in fear that we will leach of them,
But they don't know that the smallest of things, to us can equal priceless gems.
They hide their children from us when walking by,
Even when the children wave at us and say 'Hi'
They don't want us to show them how corrupt the world really is,
Instead they want to feed lies to their children, showing them the world is full of bliss.
People like us are just a nuisance in their perfect world.

They don't know...
What we would give for a warm bed during those cold sleepless nights,

How we have hearts too, that just beat in a different dim light.
They don't know...
That we would give to just have a roof over our heads,
Instead they assume we chose this life, by taking the wrong meds.
They don't know...
That if it all was reversed, we would stop by to help and give more,
Instead they choose to walk by and just ignore.

They say only time can cause change,
But how many days or years is it going to take for our deaths to stop appearing on the front page?
How many lives will be taken before they start to notice us?
When will people begin to lend help instead of making a huge fuss?

Many of us have accepted this life in utter defeat,
But I have found a way to endure this like a blazing heat.
To continue breathing while being poor and homeless is a great power,
To continue to beg for the basic necessities then to give up and cower.
So easy it is to stop the pain and hunger,
But the fact that we continue to peruse and live longer...
In my opinion, is the biggest superpower.

Amrah Janoofar (16)

Refugee

I am a koala
Furry, small
This is my story
Of how nature falls.

I once lived with luxury
Many friends, no foes
Lots of sweet leaves
And I still had my toes.

My abode was a mansion
Above the sneaky beasts
It was cosy, five star
No one expected a fiery feast.

Then at last it came
Finally the time
For my pleasure to end
It was bitter like the lime.

The wind was steaming
Things were heating up
We were the water
In your boiling cup.

Soon came the spark
That tiny little ember
Seemingly harmless
Lost its temper.

Before I knew it
Our forest was lit
Top to bottom
Every bit.

My fur was scorched
One toe burnt
I saw no sign of my parents
But lots of sleeping birds.

Before long I knew
There was no going back
I had to go ahead
And follow my own track.

I walked ahead
On my own four hands and feet
It was a long, tiring journey
But I was in the mood to beat.

Finally I found a bright place
Bustling with lots of people
I had heard it was the city
And there no one was feeble.

Yet I slowly clambered up a road
I looked out and saw a big man
I ran out looking for some help
But instead I got a chasing with a fan.

He ran after me screaming
"Vermin! Vermin! Kill it quick! Kill it quick!"
I felt the rapid fan hit me
It hit me and gave me a painful prick.

Blood streamed out from my back
I felt myself lose control
Over my body, my mind
I slumped to the ground and began to roll.

Down the road I began to go
Till I was stopped by a large black shoe
Relief flooded me, help at last
But I thought too soon; with the wind I flew.

I landed on a tree
Above the nasty men
I had a bite, finally food
But it tasted odd, not like Uncle Sven's.

Instantly I spat it all out
I scavenged the road for leaves for me
All I found was plastic and dirt
And other animals; rats and bees.

They had a similar fate
Homes wrecked
Swatted away
Never respected or fed.

I began to realise I had no choice
Nowhere to go, nowhere to hide
My fate was decided, there was no denying
I'd live in the sewers or I'd be fried.

I am a koala
Burnt, discreet
You burnt me
I went under your feet.

Tanish Kirodian (11)

The Painter's Muse

No one sees how that young girl was blind to his heart,
and had fallen deaf
due to harsh rumours of his foreboding bankruptcy;
there was no money in painting for the untrained.
However to innocent kids money mattered not.

They were free to dance in vineyards and eat in fields,
and play pretend with love.
I have not thought of when I was a girl lately.
Not for years to be truthful until my grandson
asked me to visit his gallery's exhibit.

Here I see the frames that contain that old boy's name,
and a girl, who has aged.
She has curls of copper hair flowing down her back,
flawless fair skin, honey eyes and glossy peach lips.
The vibrant plants, behind her, didn't beat her beauty.

Was that how he had seen me? How did I not know?
I had become his muse.
I had overthrown the sunset lake at autumn.
If I had known, maybe I would not have said yes
to a nobleman's loveless, regrettable ring.

I remember times of hoping he liked me too,
however I grew up,
and the ideals of money were deafening.

Despite the noise, he still painted. He painted me.
And my hopeless love was lost to natural greed.

Yet I look upon his serenity painted,
and I can remember
my sister's dress and those bracelets from the market,
and a boy, who I had once loved, unseen, painting.
He had called the painting 'the blossom of spring's love'.

Why hide from me that in your eyes there was pure love,
then paint it for the world?
That girl was cruel and made misguided mistakes.
How did he see so much grace, good and joy in me
to paint a regular day at home so divine?

Before he was my first love, he was my friend
and the friendship lingered
until that brutal golden ring ripped us apart.
Yet all I see in this gallery is one girl.
So I need to query the gallery's guide why.

Out of all the paintings of my youth on display,
she points at my wedding
and swiftly says, "Close relatives have reported
that after that one he was unable to paint
and resorted to hanging himself." I start crying
No one sees how I didn't know, how he had loved me.

Arwen Carr (16)

I See You

From head. To toe. You stare meticulously, hours on end
at me. Your reflection.
Expressionless, but confused; affirmative but hurting
Your head pounding - overflowing with the letters that made up words,
the words that made up sentences,
the very sentences they used to discard your last feeling of self-gratification.
Your eyes - restless - scanning every last detail of your gradually deteriorating figure,
locating your imperfections, amplifying them,
Not to anyone else, but to yourself.
Your legs appear strong in your mind but in reality are frail,
Frail from the mounts of pain they carved into your delicate skin,
Frail from the agonising burden of hatred you've had to endure,
Frail all because of the explicit reason that you are you.
Fingering your wounds so you'd bleed just that little bit more
to somehow tranquilise the true soreness you feel,
the anger that you feel,
You don't want to believe them but your face tells it all.
It may sound dubious, yet I see more of you than you see in yourself,
I see everything.
The blemishes, the euphoria, even when you're afraid to show it.

I see it when you start to believe the lies caressed into your amiable little mind
and I see it when you don't.
Surely somewhere you can find an ounce,
an inch of yourself that you can learn to love.
And once you do, nurture it,
allow it to grow till that very same inch flourishes.
But don't stop there.
There is more of you to love than to hate.
You see the surface of the iceberg,
I see the strong foundation beneath the water.
You see the minuscule flower beginning to bloom,
I see the roots from the germinated seed.
You see yourself skin deep,
but I see the beauty within and beneath.
From head. To toe.
You stare meticulously, hours on end
at me. Your reflection.
But the difference now is you know your worth is far deeper than just words.

Jasmeen Banya (15)

Dear Readers Of This Poem

When I say that I feel trapped in a jar,
please realise that I need your comfort or I'll scar.
The ground shakes and starts rotating around me,
tumbling and stumbling, they won't let me flee.

Readers of this poem, have you ever experienced such great pain,
that all you feel is your body trapped with an iron chain?
The poison of their words always inject my heavy thoughts,
in fact I'd much rather have the pain of gunshots.

Readers of this poem why do you stand there in silence,
suddenly overwhelmed by a new-found shyness?
Oh wait! I forgot, it's because I'm not worthy of your help,
either that or because you're too fearful they'll make you yelp.

Readers of this poem what use is it in comforting me,
when you join in with the jeering, leaving me screaming like a banshee.
It hurts me more since I know that they won't stop,
never, not unless they hear the steady footsteps of a cop.

Readers of this poem, I moved far away from the drum,
yet their taunting voices haunt me, making me numb.
Then all of sudden, I feel like I'm plunged into an ice-cold river,
Even though its 117 °F, I'm left there to shiver.

Readers of this poem, stop saying I'm over-reacting
because I'm not and believe me when I say that I'm not acting.
All I want to do is to be able to expunge,
expunge all my memories that make my heart lunge.

Readers of this poem, this didn't have to happen
next time all you have to do is step in, next time all you have to do is stop them,
I pray you have taken something away from this poem,
it's never too late to help stand up for someone.

Dear readers of this poem, *please* stand up to bullying.

Arani Ganeshwaran (14)

Mother Earth

Our Earth,
Is like a bird,
Flying low,
Until the last blow,
Good or bad,
Makes it sad,
There's never love,
Let alone a dove,
It isn't bold enough,
And in the cold will cough,
It would perish and rot,
If It's burning hot,
And just right,
Is not a sight,
With mere survivals,
Against we ravenous rivals,
If only we,
Were able to see,

Our Earth,
Is like a bird,
Flies high,
And never will die,
Resting on a bough,
To watch the show,
It can go anywhere,
Without a care,

Stands tall and lean,
Like a queen,
But reality is yet to be seen,

Our world is cursed by man,
Who is evil and hasn't a fan,
All the species,
Shed their faeces,
In his presence,
As he is a murderous menace,
He kills all,
And drinks alcohol,
He has no use,
And does abuse,
He cuts down trees,
And then he flees,
He says it's hazy,
But is actually just lazy,
But is charged with fuel,
For the sake cruel,
He goes to the till,
And then takes the pill,
But we can change it with our will.

Mother Earth, Mother Earth,
Swearing upon you lovely hearth,
We shall plant some evergreen trees,
For the sake of nature's glee,

From man's cruel canes,
And deadly pains,
I hope this not to go in vain,
And the all the trees for this paper,
Should rejoice and start to merrily caper,
For this poem,
Should scare and show them,
Because what we are doing,
Must start improving,
So stop and think,
Until the brink,
For a solution,
To stop pollution,
And stop crime,
Because it's metaphorically grime,
Don't kill animals,
And start being canonical,
Help reduce global warming,
Because it isn't charming,
To stop wasting,
And start recreating,
To make Earth green,
And sparkling clean,
Start being peaceful,
And do not be dismal,
Start believing,
And start achieving,

Because this is a dream,
And is not a meme,
Because if you believe, achieve, be and see, like me,
It will be,
Reality.

Vedanta Warad (12)

You Don't Know What I've Seen

I have seen it all
Birth to death, birth to death
The endless cycle, time and time again
I have seen and know everything
That you will never know or see
Because you don't know what I've seen

I have seen humans ravage the Earth
With their ceaseless wars
And lust for wealth and power
And I have seen what war leaves behind
Grieving mothers, sobbing widows
And innocent souls now nothing more
Than names on a memorial that no one will read.
Power-hungry, tyrannical leaders
Corruption, violence, rape, murder
Forced labour, human trafficking, global warming
All the evil that ever was and ever will be
You don't know what I've seen

And yet there are other emotions too,
Joy, ecstasy, euphoria
When the war is over and we can live again
When a country is newly independent,
The old rulers finally overthrown
Or something as simple
As a happy child

Running freely in their own little world
Birth, marriage, homecoming, togetherness
Nature, art, music, dance
All the beauty that the Earth has been filled with
You don't know what I've seen

Apart from the two extremes
Of pure joy and the depths of despair
There are countless other occurrences that I have witnessed
The rise and fall of empires
The beginning and end of dynasties
The discovery of gravity
The invention of the telephone
The devastating creation of nuclear weapons
The amazing creation of aviation,
Opening the skies to all
All that has happened and ever will happen
You don't know what I've seen

What am I?
You might wonder
As I begin to describe what I have seen
How can I have seen
All that I claim to have seen?
I tell you this
What can have seen
All that has happened in all time

Except for time itself
For I am Time
And Time is me
And you will never know what I've seen

Neha Narne (12)

Being Simone Biles

Standing tall ready to face the knife-edge,
I feel tension in the crowd before me,
Like the pinballs on a game machine waiting to be released,
Yet I am determined, daring and driven,
This beam will not defeat me!

I flip onto the beam. My eyes are on the prize,
I twist, I spin, I leap across the platform,
I feel powerful and supersonic as I block out the crowd,
The noises, gasps and sounds of disbelief
This beam will not defeat me!

The beam is like a knife-edge,
As it stretches out before me,
The edge is sharp but familiar, I know it well.
I feel the pressure, but remember the beam is my friend
We are one!
This beam will not defeat me!

Standing on the podium, my heart is pounding so hard I feel like it will burst from my chest,
Nervous anticipation builds, the crowd is deadly silent,
I didn't want to let them down,
They believe in me,
Gold! Again! I did it, I feel unstoppable, thank you,
The beam did not defeat me!

Pollyanna Morris (12)

NHS Poem

S he was looking forward to 2020.
T he year was full of plans with lots of dates on the calendar.
A ll sorts of lovely things arranged with family and friends,
Y oung and old, people to see and places to go.

H er parents' ruby anniversary, her daughter's 16th birthday,
O ccasions, celebrations, parties and days out.
M any memories were going to be made and she was
E xcited about the year ahead.

P eople started talking about a virus and she
R ealised that it was getting serious.
O n her ward, she cared for extremely ill patients,
T reating and helping the
E lderly, who needed and trusted her.
C oronavirus was in her hospital and
T he cases were increasing day by day.

T he Prime Minister told the country to stay home.
H e asked the British people to take responsibility,
E xcept they didn't, so next came lockdown.

N ever before had she seen so many deaths,
H er family missed her, she couldn't go home.
S he was tired, sad, and scared.

S he knew the country was grateful, the Thursday evening
A pplause made her smile and feel happy for a moment. The
V irus had taken away so much and hurt so many,
E motions were strong and the future was unclear.

L ife would never be the same again and she tried to
I magine reuniting with her family, desperate to replace
V irtual hugs with real ones.
E ven though COVID-19 had changed her world,
S he had hope for a positive future with family and friends.

Callum Dickson (13)

Premature Departure

Marking the time of release,
The gentle ticking of a clock continued,
I was soon to be put at ease.

They would cry and mourn,
But they knew it would happen,
Right at dawn.

They approached my chamber,
Opening the penultimate door,
I was there for nobody to remember.

Flowers planted for the one who left,
Faces covered in salty water,
The loved one's theft.

Cold creatures took me,
Minutes were numbered now,
My death filled them with happiness, I could guarantee.

After death, began sorrow,
Crying and pain,
Until there were no tears left to borrow.

The last door,
Faces watched me as I walked up,
The unwelcoming people I would take pleasure to ignore.

Stolen away by a wicked man,
His premature departure,
It was as if away he ran.

The last stairs welcomed me,
The viewing platform for the world to spectate,
The warmth of the people watching me, even now, filled me with glee.

Eventually they would overcome,
Realising that the more they cried,
The worse the despair would become.

The slithering, cold snake, coiled around my throat,
The last few breaths I knew I would take,
My mind was afloat.

They would soon find joy,
At realising the wicked man's death would soon come,
Of all this, they would find something to enjoy.

They all stood around me,
Bickering and waiting eagerly,
This was comforting to a degree.

All the wickedness mankind can produce,
Was shown in this man,
The evils of the world show no sign to reduce,

I said nothing,
When asked for my final words,
I was happy with what I was soon to become.

They'll stare out the window,
Ready for another day,
Ready for the morning glow,

With the flick of a wrist,
He pulled on the lever,
I felt momentary bliss.
Snap.

Thomas Lynn-Gilbert

I Am Music

I am music the soundtrack to your life,
I bring the memories of your childhood, your parents, husband or wife.
I am the song that gets stuck in your hair,
I am your past, your now and your where.
I can inspire you to get out of bed,
the start of your day uplifting or dread?
My crescendos can lift you out of that gloom,
my euphoric melodies can fill your room.
I am the melody that helps you to sleep
I, the anticipation that gets you on the edge of your seat
and the need to dance to my triumphant beat.

"Where words fail, music speaks"
I am the influencer of your days and weeks.
Easing the suffering when people are apart,
with memories of loved ones once locked in your heart.
I help the swelling of the mind
and bring out happiness from within my lines.

Some songs stick and stay but with time will fade away,
replaced by a new song that makes your day.

I am music!

Lola White

Too Young

They said we would be a great generation,
Bring gratitude to everyone,
Yet here we are hidden behind a mask,
Faces caked in make-up
Crying ourselves to sleep.

Older generations look down on us,
Seeing us as a disgrace;
Addicted to phones, too tech-savvy.
We are a shame to older generations,
But why?

They say I'm too young to understand,
I shouldn't know my sexuality
I shouldn't be depressed
They say I'm too young to choose,
But we never even got a choice.

Too naive,
Too stupid,
They sit there in disgust,
Thinking they are better than us,
"We survived the war, you can go without your phone," they tell us,
Then they go and sit there on Facebook all night,
And scold you when you try and complain.

They are the ones who left us with nothing,
Destroyed our futures, just for some energy.
I may not grow up and have children,
Who knows?
The world may be in flames
Just for some energy.

They expect us to fix it,
But how can we fix their mistakes?
We are just the indifferent generation
Who are too young.

Still, they say I'm too young to understand,
I shouldn't be wearing make-up
I shouldn't have to worry
They say I'm too young for this,
And you're not fully wrong.

We are 'too young' for a lot of things,
But you still rely on us to fix our future,
If we speak up, we should not be called out,
For we should be supported as we are the future.
In the future when you see us who saved the planet, who evolved technology,
Won't you regret saying we are a disgrace, a shameful generation?
For we are the future, we are Generation Z.

Jessica Travers-Spencer (12)

Quarantined

Our parched lungs are satiated with every breath of foreign air,
We're euphoric inhaling psychedelic aromas of the outside,
We sorely yearn for Her godly breezes of nourishment,
Like shrivelled plants, deprived of lushness spring granted.

Nostalgia consumes whatever's left of our entities, like never before,
Wanderlust visits and opts to occupy our every thought,
We wear our acts of sanity like a mask, and tie the strings of deception,
Veiling monstrous faces of lunacy; such barbaric hands of isolation have sculpted.

Glaring at karma face-to-face, enraged, he scolds us,
We endeavour to find a pardon in his vengeful, merciless eyes,
A pungent scent of hope - however - still lingers,
Tender, angelic optimism blinding us from concrete, demonic reality.

We crave an unfamiliar world beyond our confined homes -
Aching in such a language of infatuation, even those plants pining for spring cannot recall,

We thirst for normality again; to sew the threads humanity itself tore,
We plead for the vibrancy of our retreated daydreams -
Longing for the ambrosial taste of utter freedom,

We plead to be reprieved of manacles that we, mankind, hooked and latched.

She feebly sings lullabies of restoration to us,
Outside: a lull drenched city,
Outside: now an unvisited stranger,
Outside: of our deranged, narrow minds.

We immerse into treacherous tides of agony,
We mistreated Mother Nature's gentle serenity since Her origin,
Yet now She's healing; her mellow greenery and luminous skies are rebirthing,
Absent of pollution, chaos and monsters that are mankind.

Dhriti Thakkar (15)

Continuous Movie With No Happy Ever After

saw the eyes of my soul
The window to deserted world
A decay and erosion takes place in my mind
Under the control of never-ending misery
I say my life's a movie with no happy ending
My soul captivated in a maze of disgrace
My heart full of woe numb it becomes pain
So even the piercing screeches in my songs
Seem like little pebbles by the beach
Forgetting the sunlight exists and floating above the ocean
Floating above the sea of pain
Floating above the lake of mistakes
While guilt consumes the hopeful soul inside.

my eyes wide awake even as the crickets sleep
Silence becomes a doom I fear to hear, to consume
So I find peace in chaos
The screams allow the loneliness to be eased
And so I escape to a world of a never-ending movie
that partakes in chaos and dismay

floating above the sea of pain
That scratches every delicate surface
I keep a poker face while my soul weeps in disgrace
Seeking hope at every corner it can find
But I am a prisoner to my guilt

The past suffocating joy under its feet
Strings collide with control
And take over my clouds
Now they weep, screech and scream
Louder than the hefty cars that beep,

every stillness on earth and every rose petal darkened
As I walk closer to the flowers
Once beauty becomes disastrous in chaos
I placed two loud animations
Ringing its interest in the hazing blues
Escaping again and again
And to find peace in melancholy of ruse
But my soul,
my eyes,
reflecting,
my woes
Feels pain like a never-ending movie, a masterpiece
With no happy ever after.

Satiya Bekelcha Bekelcha Yaya

The Geisha

I had a startlingly white face with vermillion lips
As my green tea I gracefully sip
My face is blood on fresh snow,
And yet my eyes always seem to be a-glow
Ostentatious ornaments hang off my ebony-black hair,
And I have been told I add an essence of peace to the air

I have an oval face and almond eyes,
I wear a mask; the girl within me dies
Clad in a heavy, silken kimono
An ancient tree shedding its auburn leaves, to the wind they blow
Dancing and poured sake and the sacred tea ceremony,
But that innocent girl inside me grows forever lonely

I cross a street of ancient, imperial Japan
I hide half on my face with an embroidered bamboo fan
Gazes and glances and looks follow me,
And cherry blossoms season brings many clients for me to entertain and see
I recite verses, my voice as lucid and pure as a shamisen,
My body is as free as a jay as I take to the stage again

The fragile beauty of the crescent moon shows her face,
And the primordial star twinkles in that hollow void of empty space
A beautiful and kind foreshadowing to the stygian night
I remove layers of make-up with the fading light

And restored, I am still that young, childish girl
Far from an immaculate, elusive pearl

Rosy-cheeked dawn runs across the land,
And I slip into heavy garments, for me far too grand
And soft pink petals come in and out of my view with the dappled light,
As an ode to spring, the day is becoming bright
I am a vessel of beauty bejewelled with riches
My life depends on each and every conversation happening without any hitches.

Hannah Lynch

The Journey Of The Amazon

The Journey of the Amazon
High in the Andes I meander downhill,
I clamber down the mountain's staircase.
Travelling on and on I'm beginning to gain speed,
I get to the edge full of courage, I leap, I flip and...
Splash!

Now with rapid speed, I am sprinting to the meander,
Trees loom over me, I'm surrounded by darkness.
A shining emerald leaf blowing in the breeze,
Fluttering down, slowly, slowly, slowly until it gives up.
Plenty more are in the tree, blowing happily are the leaves,
Another falls, there it goes, it lands on me in the shape of a cup.

I am a toddler,
I gurgle and hum.
I wear a blue baby suit,
As I suck my thumb.

He meanders calmly through the rainforest,
While leopards, tigers and parrots gather for a refreshing drink.
Oh the trees, so lanky and tall.
The poison dart frog lies low under a tree bright blue or vivid pink.

I am a monster,
I growl and leave scratches.
I could flood a whole village just you wait and see,
Houses will be squashed and will be left as mud patches.

I smell lush green grass as the sky grows dark,
I'm not tired, I don't stop, I carry on.
Through the night I go on skidding and sliding,
Calm and steady not knowing where I am going, nobody does.

I go far, I go fast,
Hiding my treasures in my paths.
Have I been eating too much? I thought,
I am beginning to get fat.

The further I go the wider I get,
I am slim until I finish my journey then I widen out.
This is the end of my journey. I am slowing down.
I'm going into the sea and there I'll be.

Bethany Painter (12)

Last Words

Through the eyes of COVID-19

Verdict: guilty as charged. Penalty: execution.

Sorry for grounding you at home and for destroying your prom,
Sorry for making you worry, and for stopping your travels,
Sorry for trapping and overworking you in hospitals,
Sorry for ruining politics and the economy,
Sorry for taking the lives of the ones you so dearly love.
Please forgive my crimes.
And the fact this does not rhyme.

But before you drag my name to dirt,
Recount all my murders out of pain,
And choose to laugh and jeer out of hurt,
Remember this in my reign:
I am responsible. I plead guilty.
I am not sorry. Never will I be.

I will not apologise for letting the toddler
Develop a stronger bond with her father
Who from day to night works as a lawyer.
I will not apologise for the man next door
Who seemed to ignore the world in others' eyes
Helped his neighbour who was low on food supply.
I will not apologise for finally making you value,
A handshake, a hug, and human interaction.
Never will I apologise for you spreading actions,

For spreading kindness and for spreading love,
To those around you and ultimately to yourself.
Why should I apologise when beautifully,
All of you learnt how to heal collectively?

When you jab me with a syringe
And put me down to sleep
To build up a defence against me
I only wish when you remember the year 2020
You remember it as the year you learnt to love.

Before you label me a cold-blooded murderer as a solution,
I hope through me you relearnt what it means to be human.

Jamie See

Spell Out My Name

When you're a pen you are not in control of anything,
I have never ever been able to spread an inch of one wing,
the grips of the grubby children chewing and spitting on me,
I am treated like a piece of rubbish carelessly swimming in the sea.

The ink in my ink reservoir is the blood that runs through your veins,
Each letter that you form is a crime for it is my blood that remains,
Some of us are used for letters of love or actual heartfelt stories,
But for most of us we are nameless left to rot in bins full of object bodies.

I feel like I have no identity, no personality and no face to show emotion,
Built like a robot but used differently as our ink is deadly and can cause an explosion,
I cherish the feeling of creation when I create ideas in the mind of a human writer,
Born with talent as his face lights up with ideas and passion I feel so much brighter.

I am the history and evidence of existence for the Egyptian and Cold War era,
Now history seems like an old memory that you forget, lost in a horrible error,
My ancestors and I have seen it all, I am the holder of present day and the future,

The saying is right, the future is yours to write, it is not a made-up rumour

All things have a dream whether they are big or small,
My dream is to be able to sit next to the mystical dream waterfall,
It is said to create your most wanted desire at any cost, even if it's gold,
Just remember when you pick up a pen the great power you behold.

Zara Eila Calvin (13)

The Oldest Caterpillar

Opening my eyes to a bright glittering world,
already knowing my purpose.
The sun won't be around for long,
so better get started

Day and night, its beaming rays reassure me,
there is still another day,
but another day is another day closer.

Find the green, find the leaves,
no time to waste.
But then green disappears and white takes its place.
The time has come.

I find a nook, a small pocket, to crawl inside,
but not to hide,
just to wait.
To wait for the inevitable.

And then it comes,
creeping, creeping,
with its facade of idyllic perfection,
but icier intentions,
like a boa-constrictor -
perusals then beguiles.
It has made its selection.

First my heart, it takes its beat.
Then my blood, it takes its flow.

Then my movement and I am paralysed in its frigid embrace.
But does it know, it has not caught me yet?

I feel it retreating.
My heart, again, starts a-beating,
and out I go, out into the light.

Find the green, find the leaves,
no time to waste.
But then green disappears and white takes its place.
The time, again, has come.

Now I am old,
the oldest caterpillar.
Seven years it has been
Since I told, told you of my monotonous gestations,
my fatal preparations.

But here I am, at the finish line,
spinning, spinning,
spinning my way to another life.
A short one maybe,
but one that will fill,
fill the deep hole that I have been creating for all these years.
A hole that I will fly out of with my soft wings...

Mia Rock (13)

Miss Maya Ro

The navies, royals, cadets and blizzards
Blend within the skies.
Wisps of pastels blush in their high heavenly spirits,
And Aquarius announces another new arrival.
Rays and beams engulf me in the fresh, crisp hope
Of another step,
Of another decision,
Of another page writing my future.
Celestial paradise of the imminent mystical magic
Carry me away in the breeze of warmth. Yet

Burdens weigh down on my shoulders. Again
Miss Maya Ro flurries in with the flush of Heaven's tears.
Pelting down on the bubbly, bustling streets of Copacabana
It leaks the black tar of Hell.
Oozing toxics, snuffing the candle out of our
- lives.
Forever.
She invites us to her home.
Infiltrates our purity, manipulating our innocence with her devious treats,
Snatching education away from right under our noses.
Beckoning us to join her army of spirits.

Aquarius blows the conch one last time.
Time had arrived for the dreaded day.
Time had arrived for the unforgiving journey.

Time had arrived for the everlasting
- pain.
Bags sink under their eyes.
Hands drag their eyes further in, creating forlorn looks.
- death.
Sweat trickles down their face.
- paleness.

There is a buzz in the air.
- look up.
There she is.
Her eyes gleam in the storm welling up behind her.
The glassy stare.
The cold mist of her breath steams on us.
My breath. My spirit coils out of me; sucked into holes of her eyes.
El dia de los muertos. Hoy.
- Help me.

Tushita Gupta

Kelly-Green Shoes

Those Kelly-Green Shoes were shipped to her
By some aunt who lived over the sea.
The dyed satin was faultless,
And the shoes unsullied from

Wearing them about the linoleum tiles,
In the kitchen before her first dance.
When the night chased the dawn,
How those soles had been worn.
Speckles of rum and Coke:
Split the dye

Split the seams,
Of those maternity jeans.
Feet gone from size five to too bloated
For means - of standing,
And so ces petites chaussures
Were laid down at the wardrobe's corner.
Broken but beloved, malodorous and marked.

Taken out of that place
Buffed up and anew,
For funerals of aunts over the sea
Yet a few christenings too.
Those children are growing, then all too soon grown.
Those children are leaving, for seas
That stretch far beyond the isles of her life,
Still down the phone echoes their woes and their strife.

The grandfather clock that shadows the hall -
Circles tick circles, time changes,
How the tempo beats faster when you wish it to stop
Those Kelly-Green Shoes dance along
Right 'til she drops.

Her family took the Fishguard Ferry at twelve:
The horses walk slowly with heads that are
Bowed, fierce rain hurling their sides.

Now out of the coffin,
At the door to the skies,
She stands - feet together -
In burnished sun and the dry.

Join the light on the heather,
With green shoe from green isle.
For aged is satin and leather,
Yet aged not is her smile.

Faye-Marie Dyke (17)

Social Media Is A Social Lie

The biological factor of the new generation is the urge and desire to fit in,
The addiction of gaining likes,
views whilst abiding to the Internet cultivate look
which is only achievable through FaceTune
and soon you're on a hook,
You're in a religion, the precision to follow trends through a lens.
But really you have no interest and pretends to like the popular craze. Sacrificing your life as you slowly gain social anxiety as your character decays.
But the connection to your phone is so strong that you're getting high off of love hearts and comments.
In them moments who need friends when you have a following.
But you're hollow, you lose sense of reality.
Becoming an illusionist
creating a world in which one doesn't exist.
Your hips are not that width,
you don't have abs but beautiful rolls and your promoting abnormality.
It's a shame as people's personality is hidden due to this new mentality... you're no celebrity, nor do you need to try to be.
Just because you have lumps, bumps and insecurities doesn't mean you're ugly.
You can still have real buddies.

Exploring the world through vision should be everyone's mission.
Not being stuck in the social prison:
Social media is a lie and we should all say goodbye.

Grace Jenman (17)

The Truth Behind The 'Happy' Friend

'You'll be fine!' people say,
But they have never felt this way,
The overthinking, the pain, the ache
All you need is one more 'you're fine' until you break,
You keep your emotions bottled up inside,
The amount of times you have cried,
Just to put on an act the next day,
And act like everything is okay.

You hide behind a fake smile,
No one understands you for a while
Until it's too late,
They don't want to be your mate,
You have no one, they were all fake,
They all show their true colours when you are about to break.

You finally open up to someone, looking for advice,
Turns out they aren't that nice,
You go home, locking yourself alone,
You find yourself in the zone,
You ask yourself 'Should I do it?' You think you have no one.

You wish all this could just be undone,
You wake up the next day,
Knowing you should stay,
You listen to an influencer,
They were right where you were,

They are so happy now,
They never let anyone bring them down.

You find someone you can trust,
You adjust
Knowing you have someone to talk to,
They know what it's like, they are just like you,
You find yourself feeling better,
You get a letter,
To improve your mental health,
You no longer have to hide your true self,
You feel reassured, knowing you are going to be okay,
Now that you know there are many that feel the same.

Millie Webb (13)

Her

Her flesh is fragile, paper-thin
as my fist paints black and blue upon her skin.
In foresight, nothing but crimson liquid reflected
from the sight of the wound I had inflicted.
I damaged a diamond, an angel, a star that shines
Brighter than blinding explosive grenades of anger in the depth of my mind.
Blinding my judgement, speech and unforgivable actions.

I didn't mean to curse her.
I didn't mean to leave her with shackled ghosts of the past
tormenting her with our past transactions:
Of screams and silent cries and her sorrow-filled walks after our fights at night.
I loved her, my second soul.
Once content unaware of the death-marked love
unaware that she would be a friend to the clay in the London ground
and would join the chimes of angelic harmonies up above.

Her pale pink, flushed, freckled skin
Now grey and decayed and white as bone.
Her thick flannel-slacked legs
now purged from meat and toothpick-thin.
Her once hazel eyes where in the depths her cries did lie
now all I think of is maggot-filled eyes.

Her lasso, her golden locks that slaved me
I want them back. I do! I plea!

Now I sit entrapped in bars
thinking of what future could have been ours.
Knowing the wrongs I caused in acts of red and green
Take me back to our first date scene -
where I can do this all again but right this time.

Paige Jasper (17)

Just Savour The Moment

The feeling of walking through the tunnel
thinking of the moments that lead up to this final
walking out knowing that win or lose, what matters is the enjoyment
just savour the moment.

Out on the pitch now shaking hands
pulling up the captain's armband
it is now time to chant our nation's anthem
just savour the moment.

the whistle's been blown and there goes the first kick
the ball is whizzing around from player to player
just watching it might make you feel dizzy or sick
now on the ball and taking it forward
this is the chance and *goal!*
The cheers, pleasure and ovation
just savour the moment.

After half-time the whistle's blown again
This time the opposing nation getting this half underway
Past one defender, past two
Looks like they're on a counter-attack
They take the shot and it slips through the keeper's hands
Oh no!
1-1, now thinking about what was said at half-time
we need to read between the lines
they are weaker on the left side

so that is our advantage
running up the left wing
10 seconds pending
The ball flies into the box and... *goal!*

The winning goal has been scored
And there goes the whistle for the end
Now standing on the podium
Medals dangling from our necks
We lift the trophy with great content
Just savour the moment.

Jonathan Nkenge (12)

The Four Siblings

Winter sleeps under the tall green pines,
She reads in a blanket of snow,
She's cooled by wind and warmed by fire,
Winter's laugh will come and go

Winter cries from icy eyes,
Her laughter makes snow thaw to rain
She wears a dress of tall green pines
She waits for them to grow again

Spring shyly peeks through the chestnut trees
She shyly springs in her coat of clover
She shyly yearns what she can never have
The sunlight of her elder sister

She bursts in, in a riot of colour
And quickly fades away
As tiny blades of green grass grow
She leaves behind a flower bouquet

Summer is the eldest,
And shines bright and carefree
She's always been the boldest
And she always will be

Daisies adorn her buttercup hair
Sunlight ripples round her feet
But in a flash her mood can change
Her hot-headed glare is hard to beat

Autumn is the quiet sister,
Moods that change like twisting winds
Golden leaves and drooping flowers
Clouds that cried and suns that grinned

Some days she is quiet and grey
Some days she shines, bright and loud
Her crown is made of leaves and branches
Clouds wrap around her like a shroud

These four siblings come and go,
In a carousel they move
Some call them seasons, but who can tell
If they are siblings too?

Manasvi Kommuri (13)

I Miss My Mother

I miss my mother, she was stolen from me
They are holding her captive, why can't they see
That I can't be left alone, I am only a baby
They will give her back soon, just maybe

I have seen other monkeys survive on their own
But without my mother there is nowhere to call home
Every day my home gets ruined or cut down
So every day I am forced to move around

My mother guided me so without her it is hard
I don't know how to forget this, for life I will be scarred
I am afraid of the days and nights still to come
As I know they will be agonising without my mum

All of the time, every day
They cut down trees and I continue to pray
For a better future and for peace on Earth
Because I know that families shouldn't be separated at birth

They locked my mother in a cage
I am afraid she won't be here to see me age
Every day I cry and moan
That I will no longer be alone

200,000 acres of rainforest gets destroyed every day
We need to act fast and make a change

Without trees we are polluting what we are trying to breathe
Clean air has been stolen and we are the thieves.

Lily Johnson (13)

World In Colour

My left eye opens to half a world soaked in colours.
My right eye opens to half a world drained of colours.
For the first time, I see the world before me
For the first time, I see the world through my eyes.

I watch, aimless wondering.
I watch, focused running
I watch, as people draw their final breath.
I watch, as people draw a breath closer to their last.

A canvas overflowing with blues, browns, yellows, oranges, reds, greens.
A spectacle to one's eye. Lively and life itself.
A forest of curiosity, a desert of lost hope.

Through my eyes I see views change,
Mountains layered with snow, rivers and streams flow.
A soft quiet breeze or a harsh pounding breeze.

Through my eyes I see views change,
Eyes that see hatred, eyes that see fear
Eyes that spill water, eyes that know of cheer
Eyes the colour of buttercups, eyes like glistening stars.

Through my eyes I see all.
Blue April showers, yellow spring sunflowers, red embers in mid-Decembers, green overgrown grass in summers.

Through everyone's eyes I see colour.
Some are brighter and some much duller.
Through eyes I see hope, through eyes I see retreat
And once again I will repeat, through my eyes I see all.
A world half in colour, a world half in shade.

Evelyn Thomas

My Life Working For The NHS During COVID-19

The life I want I'm wanting more
the way I go is unsure
but I'm unready I am unsteady,
and I don't know where I'm going.

But I'm finally ready, the time has come
to flap my wings and reach the sun,
then disaster strikes, a plague hit the world
with an iron fist we all cowered and curled.

I'm working every second to save innocent lives from an untimely fate
but people are dropping at an unthinkable rate.
Why? Why? Why is the world so unfair?
This is more than I can bear.

Why can't people listen and stay in their homes?
Live their lives on the inside
and hide away from this terrible sickness?
More and more with no cure.
The dark clouds hanging over my eyes as the days repeat themselves
My future is unsure.

2020 has brought the worse in all.
The greed will lead to our eventual downfall.
Why? I ask.

Why has this devastation hit our world?
Some say karma, some say revenge
but either way I want it to end.

There's a spark of light in distance.
Hope, the beacon that's shining down with no resistance
I believe they'll see the light I see
and I'll help every person I can,
and everything will go according to plan.

Lily Hills (12)

Puppet In Shackles

That night we went out,
Bowling,
A girl sat sadly,
By the wall.
I didn't mind her,
But they did,
And they implored me,
To insult her,
To hurl those words,
That stuck like pollen to flower.
I played my part,
And bellowed those words,
That shed her heart,
Into pieces,
And flooded her eyes.
My friends sniggered,
And offered me a trophy,
One I wanted so bad,
That I couldn't resist.
A small taste of regret,
It wasn't that bad.
Was it?
But no matter how many times,
I pull away,
The chains control my limbs,
Like a puppet on strings.

I tried to cut the cords,
But always knew,
The manacles would bite and strangle harder,
Until I collapse on the edge,
Of the cliff of instant death.
The bullying isn't me,
I am the empty puppet,
Seized on shackles of hatred,
And greed.
The bullying really is not me,
I try to tear and gnaw at the cuffs,
But it is hopeless.
The bullying is honestly not me,
They shape me,
Don't they?
And play with me,
Like a doll,
Do they not?
But now I see,
The bullying is me,
I choose to do it,
I can't go back.
The whirlpool of regret,
Getting bigger and bigger.
Until it releases,
And is then ready to bite back,
To all those people who cuffed me.

Kairi Savage (11)

Australian Bush Fires

As I sat in the back of the firetruck, I could see the fires blazing outside, burning down the trees brushing everything else aside.

The giant orange flames swallowing up the land, destroying people's property
but my job is to stop that,
to save people's lives,
to fight off the giant orange flames destroying all the land.

As I jumped out of the truck fully suited in fire gear and helmet
the heat was like no other,
not any a man could stand.

As I looked into the flames, I felt scared and unprepared about what was about to happen,
the pain that would be felt if I was never to return.

I thought about family and friends to help spur me on,
to help me to know I will return,
and I won't be gone.

I could smell the smoke and burning coming from the trees,
as I sprayed water
into the flames from the giant hose I held.

I could barely see a thing as the smoke got thicker and thicker
as if creating a wall from the terrible destruction that I was not yet ready to see,

but it is what it is,
and my job is to stop that,
to save people's lives,
to fight off the giant orange flames destroying all the land.

Adam Atkins (12)

The Cell

In my walls a prisoner stands,
Bombing all around us,
He never leaves,
No one ever enters.

Silence engulfs the months,
I cannot gather the voice to speak,
Though would have much to say,
Bars of steel are not a good mouth,
To express my words.

Though one day a man comes,
He takes out a key,
Open my bars,
For the first time in months,
My prisoner is not alone.

The words of the other,
Make my face glow,
To hear a flood of words again,
I listen in to the conversation.

The phrases withered once more,
To stay another year this man,
Had to go along alone,
With only silent me beside him.

Slowly, slowly over the year,
With only stale bread and water,

He began to stink something awful,
He lost his mind,
And rotted slowly from the inside.

A cold form against my wall,
The man's soul had left him,
All of a sudden I felt empty,
Never before had I felt so connected,
To one I had enclosed within me.

Never again will I be so distraught,
About a measly prisoner,
Silent tears fell down my face,
Until the next mortal comes,
On my own I shall be.

Wait, is that footsteps I hear?
Tears, a screaming voice crying out,
The mother of my long friend,
Together we mourn till the end.

Jessica Williamson (13)

The Power Of Internalized Racism

I am the face of the race,
You won't understand me until you climb into my skin,
And then walk around in it,
Every time I look at society,
I am infected with anxiety,

They squeezed tears out of my stinging eyes,
Look at me as if I'm disabled,
Trying to avoid being labelled,
I ain't part of a tribe,
Why you giving that vibe,

Back to the present,
I see no changes,
All I see is racist faces,
Misplaced hate makes disgrace for races we under,
I wonder what it takes to make this world a better place for the monotonous race,

My parents hid me from reality,
Distanced me from culture,
Because of their past,
They should've known it wouldn't last,
This triggered my frantic emotions,
Feeling compelled for retribution so I defied them for the first time,
Went to the south as the raven cawed,
The petrifying tranquillity shattered,

As intolerable repulsion lingered in the air,
It took two days for them to find out,
They couldn't breathe,
As they didn't want to believe,
That distancing me from reality,
Could create monstrosity to an extent that was... was unfathomable, truly inconceivable.

Rayan Bhuiyan

I Am Standing With A Crestfallen Feeling

Everybody wears happy faces,
Smiling and going around without distress.
Oh, I wish I could wear that fake mask.
To cover my melancholic eyes, hiding it is not an easy task.

Everybody is singing and laughing, without a care
that someday they might lose everything.
Oh, I wish I don't have this overthinking mind.
I don't wanna see sad and humiliated faces - after being cheerful and kind.
I don't wanna see them fall;
I don't wanna see them burst in tears and crumble.

Everybody is whispering and consoling their exhausted souls.
Tapping each other's back, hoping it will extinguish the burning coals.
Oh, I wish I had an enchanting voice.
I don't wanna see them at 3am, drowning in tears,
for they are left with no choice.

Everybody seems to be sad.
Oh, my bad.
Everybody tells everything about me.
Everybody is no one else, but me.
The mirror never tells a lie.

The fake smile,
the deceiving laughter,
the deafening songs,
the false optimism,
they were all lies.
Now, I'm standing with river-like eyes.
Slowly breaking as humiliation stabs me.
But I am still standing with a crestfallen feeling.

Althea Beliran (16)

The Sea

The pounding waves upon the shore,
The ocean's great and mighty maw,
Gobbling wood and steel and flesh,
Every day to start afresh,
Lost to the sea forever,
Rhythm ceasing never,
'Til it all is dust.

Countless vessels both small and large,
From titanic warship to humble barge,
Now lie salt-encrusted, innate,
Left to their wretched fate:
Lost to the sea forever,
Rhythm ceasing never,
'Til the boats are but dust.

An almighty ocean, claiming lives,
Caring nought but who survives,
Seeking vengeance and dealing woe,
To all decided as a foe,
Lost to the sea forever,
Rhythm ceasing never,
'Til their bones are dust.

The ocean's vast and gaping maw,
Now filled with plastic from shore to shore,
The coral reefs, islands, beaches,
None escaped our far-flung reaches.

Lost to us forever,
Despite any endeavour,
'Til we are but dust.

The crunching stones beneath my feet,
The salty air, both tangy and sweet,
Cool calm waves caressing the sand,
The sun disappearing behind the land,
Lost to the sea forever,
Rhythm ceasing never,
'Til a new day dawns.

Ruth Sloper (12)

The Vulnerable

People buy in times that are vile,
The food they stockpile.
It rots away,
And they cry "Hooray!"
As they take more food for the safety in feeling bold,
When the fresh fruit turns to mould.
This continues in a circle,
And the rotten food they hurtle,
Into the trash,
And then stock more in their stash.
Now imagine you have a family member,
You shared good times together, remember?
But they are vulnerable,
And they can't go out because they are vulnerable,
They rely on a rare online slot,
Which are gone as food is taken and left rot.
The people who stockpile,
Make this time even more vile.
Your loved one is left alone,
Because of the people that own,
A stash of rotting food,
While loved ones starve (how very crude).
Do you have a stash?
Then throw the mould in the trash?
Please I beg, oh please,
If you stockpile then cease!

Only take what you need,
So those in need can feed.
Do this for all families
In calamities.
You have the power,
So every hour,
Remember your community,
Show some care for those with least immunity.
It is down to you
And thank you.

Alfie Reece Conal Wilson (13)

Barn Owl

Wait! What's that?
My muscles are tense,
Could it be dinner - a vole or a rat?
Piercing eyes slice through the dark,
Scanning the surface as my pupils dilate,
Talons sharpened I push off the bark,
My mind is busy with a mish-mash of thoughts
This could be the final chance to survive,
My brain is a whirlpool - what creature have I sought?
And then...
Silence.
I glide from the perch,
As elegant as a dancer, like a leaf in the breeze
My soft feathers twitch, I begin my search,
Can I hear something beneath the snow?
Beginning a descent I swoop with one flap,
Hoping no one will notice my ghostly glow,
Predator mode on - two more feet
Heightened senses in overdrive
I can almost taste the succulent meat.
Perfect landing, straight through the frost
Brain freeze - wait for senses - but,
My heart collapses as I think what I have lost
I feel sick with disappointment and disgust,
There's nothing wedged in a beak nor skewered on a claw,
Will my precious chicks lose their trust?

I'm almost beyond caring by the time I get back
But wait! What's that?

Evelyn Edwards (12)

How Can They Just Stand There?

How can they just stand there?
Ignoring what we do
Not giving us the respect that we deserve
When they could never do what we do
They could never stand at the front
They just flock to the back
With no wish for a better world,
The world in which we live.

How can they remain quiet?
Ignoring the screams
Not acknowledging anything other than their own thoughts
When we are out there for their safety
They could never utter these words
Because they will never do
Anything that might help the world,
The world in which we live.

How can they be immune to this insanity?
Ignoring the pain
Not caring if they break everything we have worked for
Shutting out anything and everything that might hurt us
Even when we are dying
They just do not care
For anything in this world,
The world in which we live.

How can they live like this?
Lost, forgotten, alone
Not wanting to find a better solution
Soulless and desolate their bodies and minds remain
Although they think themselves beyond saving
They do not seem to mind
About anyone else in this world,
The world in which we live.

Libby Pearse (13)

Far Away

Clinging to my skin is the mask
which steals my strangled breath
as I complete the daily task
Of going to market to
haggle a lower price,

And yet the smog grips my chest like an
Iron vice.
Men are shouting, women begging,
pegging clothes through which I steal a route.

2096 and still no sign
of the situation being fixed. Two men
break out a row with handheld signs stating
polluting everything
and
what happened?

But it's all well and good
if you're young like me,
at least that's what
They say. But I'm choking on my thoughts
and words and the situation's futility.

I returned home. What did you get?
Fruit, milk, a loaf of bread...
And a lung infection,

the lot of them said.
I don't feel the need to hang my head.

2021 is rolling in, a juggernaut;
and yet I'm sat here on the kerb, reading this book
which claims to predict the future in its thoughts.
And as I close the leather spine, look over the city
which doesn't feel like mine,
I think maybe it's not so far away.

Because the nightmare seems to be today.

Abi Bartlett

Painted Reality

I wish I could see what other people see
I wish the world was bright and colourful
I wish I looked like other people
Oh yes I know it will never come to be
How I feel is completely up to me
But you, oh you
The version I want to be
I'm scared, insecure and to be honest...
99.99% of the time I let myself cry.
Over humanity and the cruel reality,
The voice in the back of my head says,
"Something should really be said."
If actions speak louder than words
Then why war? Why bully? Why neglect? Why suffer? Why harm?
The most advance generation creating the most destruction
To the mind and to the future
The reality I wish to be requires delicacy, time, patience and optimism
Yet I'm a rushed and corrupt painting
Fix me please fix me
Sew up my canvas.
Now 'fixed' and never the same again
I'm ready for the next generation's sins in the form of bullets and anger
To penetrate my surface again and again until I can no longer be fixed.

Only then will there be peace and utter silence.
But not the version I wish to be.

Joelle Delta Williams (15)

The Wind Blows By

The wind blew by as I was rooted to my spot,
My leaves waved hi to the people across,
They all stared at me, a glare of daze,
Some turned away, looking at the sky,
That seemed to go grey among them, up high.

The breeze blew slow,
Spring was here, as it came with a glow,
My leaves came back with a ray of hope,
Happiness flourished bigger than the sky,
As it illuminated,
Beyond what may come, during time.

The gust of wind blew at a speed,
Summer was here, as I had envied,
My leaves had thrived,
Bigger than before,
As they stayed on tight,
It was a galore of pride,
As there was nothing to hide.

A strong breeze blew by,
My leaves were crumpled,
Autumn was here, as it came with a dark flow,
My colour had faded; leaves were dying,
I was standing alone for a better tomorrow.

The blizzard blew hard as my branches were still,
Winter was here, as it came with a chill,
My leaves were gone, my pride had vanished,
Nothing to hide, yet I stood alone.

As spring blooms,
As summer runs,
As autumn flies,
As winter implies,
The beginning of hope
The wind blows by.

Sanah Sygle (12)

Murder Mile

This is it.
They've taken a headshot of my face.
Death dished by a drive-by. I see sky.
That's a real blue story
I made the wrong move on Murder Mile
Now my body is guarded by powdered chalk
I know these flashing lights too well.
I fell in love with quick cash
so quickly that it spun to cold cash
It seems selfish but all I wanted was an ice cheque
It's funny - it started with counting everlasting money
Then overstepping the line,
Pow!
Suddenly, I'm working for county lines
And I get caught in postcode crossfires
And then I really play with God
Because I attend church
All the while I repent. Sin. Repent. Sin
I promise evil does not run through my veins
I am another one of God's lost souls,
I am another youth that couldn't find their way back home
That adapted to the crime,
That adapted to the poverty
I don't expect you to understand.
Our lives do not correlate
because as soon as my skin turns grey

and this stone road absorbs my blood
I am yet another youth plastered on the news.

Jasmine Balind-Ayoola (16)

Selection

His eyes were on the back of my head like sirens
Waiting to alert at any minute
He was carving deep into my body each second
Chip
Chip
Chip
I couldn't let him
I had to stay focused
This was the most important day of my life
Selection
If I didn't get chosen then it was all over
If I didn't get chosen then it was all for nothing
The betrayal, the disloyalty, the heartbreak
His eyes rested on the back of my head
I couldn't show any signs of weakness
I couldn't let him ruin everything
I wasn't going to let him
My broad shoulders lifted to face my opponent
This was it, who was it going to be?
I prowled forward, not losing eye contact
He stood his ground, snarling, ready for a fight
Soon we reached each other and his hot breath swept over me like steam
Our jaws clenched in sync as a small crowd gathered to watch

My mind was ready, my body was ready
Who was going to make the first move?

Esther Higgins Mcvey (14)

Emotion Cloak

Expressionless. Completely utterly expressionless.
Presenting my emotions to humankind is a felony.
Blank as a thin sheet of paper delicate like my emotions.

I can't be alone with my tears of emotions, I can't handle them.
I can't be alone with my fears of emotions becoming visible; for the world to see.
I just can't

Embarrassed. Completely utterly embarrassed.
My cold droplets flow like the nostalgic pain growing through my thin hot veins.
I can't be alone with my thoughts

It's my worst nightmare.
I'm a hostage of emotion.

Afraid. Completely utterly afraid.
Why did things have to be this way?
Can they hear my defeat?

They've won.

My emotions have destroyed my rational thoughts.

Why am I trying to express myself?
How do I express myself?
Can't you see I'm trying to express myself?
How do I fight my emotions myself?

Or have I fallen into the misleading traps of my thoughts and emotions?

I can't escape
I can't fight my fear
I just can't.

Britney Limbaya Basuama (15)

The Big, Round And Blue Earth

As I look out the 16-inch thick glass.
I see my reflection and the big, round and blue Earth.
It hits me.
No seriously, the glass hit me.
Then it really hits me: that my descent has begun.

The round, big and blue Earth gets closer.
The white-as-marshmallow clouds get bigger.
The futuristic screen is beeping 'atmosphere'.
The indescribable view gets reddish.

The approaching purple sea is daunting.
The dolphins and whales are passing.

Whoosh!
And then a sudden yet expected stop.
I stop praying and look out.
The blue, big and round Earth still at least 20 miles below.

And the vivid parachute is out
However, the parachute's strings are looking oddly like noodles.
Flailing about in the air like that.

An eternity later we land and I think that I'll never experience zero gravity again.

I'll never experience the overwhelming adrenalin when you see the Earth.
The 16 sunsets and sunrises.

"I'm back you big, round and blue Earth."

Dhruv Maheshwari

Dementia

Rock, rock, rocking on a chair.
Staring at an endless void.
Alone in a dark attic
his fuzzy mind shuts the artificial light

The skylight a beam, projecting
a fluttering memory,
a butterfly hard to catch.
No net nor grip can grasp it.

A swirling tornado tickling his brain
when he holds out his hand
feeble and hopeful - he grabs at it.
It pixelates away. Slips through his fingers.
Returns briefly, to draw a smile
then dissipates for good.

  L ove dances boisterously and steals the hollow heart
  O ver her face a mask. Her words sweet, so
  V ery sweet, but his heart fluttered pivoting.
  E ndlessly cheating the mind, deceiving the blind

As snippets of life prance before his eyes
He holds the photograph, rusty with decay
The edges withered as
his memories fly away

A paper chain, twisting tightly at his wrist
With only the barcode on it to keep him sane

And the photo resting on his lap
He dozes off on his
Rock, rock, rocking chair.

Hiba Mohamed Efhil (15)

I Suffer Ashes

The forest is speaking to me
It whispers soothingly
I hide in its branches
And listen to its secrets
Lost in its green veins until

A voice of gravel and coals
The shouts. The cries.
I rush to the safety of the treetops
I see, now.
They're in my forest
The scream of gears and chains
The roar of a chainsaw kills the peace
Trees shatter into broken shards
They tear it away as if it was nothing
Twisting through the undergrowth
They hunt and harvest
In the path they make nothing is safe
They kill.
And nobody seems to notice

Death rains
The sky is black
Is this punishment?

The orange glow
I have been doused in gasoline
You took a match to me

Now I suffer ashes
Scars tear themselves into my orange folds
They rip and scramble across my flesh

My home -
My house is on fire.

There was once,
Once upon a time
A forest
A garden of eternity
Where -
Nobody listens. Nobody cares.
You didn't listen. You didn't care.
It has gone
It is dust
It has been blown away.

Noah Robinson (16)

Lost To Be Found

Hey angel,
I see you,
Those salty drops pouring from your eyes,
Your walls crashing down,
And I hate to see it,
How do I hold you up when you watched me be put down?
I hear you my poor child,
Your muffled sobs drench your pillowcase,
Your silent screams penetrate through my soul,
Your empty heart,
Your world turning black and blue,
My death being untrue to you,
But please my Isabella,
You are strong,
So please breakthrough,
We are apart now,
But I'll see you soon,
I love you my little flower,
I'm watching you bloom.

Hey Mum,
I feel your presence sometimes,
It feels loving and warm,
So please heal me,
I ache in pain like flames burning in my heart,
Your absence hurts,
I'm drowning,

Replace my inner demons with peace,
And fill the dark hole that leaves me restless at night,
You were my butterfly but now you have been set free,
I can't wait to see you soon,
Tell you how I have been,
In hopes to taste your sweet, sugary tea.
Lost to be found.

Zainab Soogun

The Blue Whale

As you know,
I am the big blue whale.
I'm an endangered species,
Longer than a bus or a sail.

We then became so famous,
That some people tried to kill us.
They killed us for our meat,
And apparently we were delicious.

They never stopped,
And so they caused more damage.
All caused, by those human savages.

And so we left,
We fled and we tried.
But we realised,
That we were denied,
And were facing genocide.

Our world is the water,
And our home is the depths of the sea.
We only came up,
When it was necessary.
But if we did,
The world above us was still frightening and scary.

So now you know our story,
And how it would be seen.

How scary the humans,
And their minds can be.

But we're still huge and famous,
So you have to come and save us.
Hurry or you'll be too late,
Or the humans will decide our fate.

And even if you don't tell the people these atrocities,
The only thing stronger than fear is curiosity.

Save the blue whale!

Noor Haque Prieto (12)

The Perfect Life

I'm a teenage girl,
It's difficult at times.
But you find a way around it,
At least that's what they think!

School, friendship and education,
They expect you to get it all right.
But little do they know,
The truth to it all...

You start young,
But then you notice changes.
The opinion of everyone else,
Which is sacred to our reputations.

Body image and controversy,
Starving yourself for that perfect body.
We want to look like those celebrities,
But it's not always that easy.

We compare ourselves,
Stare in the mirror for hours.
That fake smile,
Which fools everyone to think we are fine.

Those friends you think are real,
But one day they will stab you.
Trusting the wrong people,
Then having to hear all those rumours.

"It's okay, you'll get over it"
Fed up of hearing that?
Well if not, it's fine,
Because you aren't getting any other advice.

The world behind our eyes,
Which is a myth to everyone else...

Tanisha Kaur (13)

Grandparents

I lie awake at night,
thinking about you.
Will you stay safe,
or will the monster get you?

So kind, yet so weak,
So generous, yet so fragile,
So caring, yet so vulnerable.
But it doesn't care, does it?

It rakes across the land,
slaying everything in its path.
Fuelled by hate and evil,
all you can do is wait.

Wait in a cage of loneliness,
Wait for salvation and help.
But I know you have hope,
You will never give up.

Tears roll down my face,
Sorrow lies in my heart.
Despair and powerless wrap around,
I would give anything to see you again.

To feel the flame of warmth in your hugs,
To bask in the abundance of your kindness.
I know you are always there,
For me beyond forever.

Please, don't turn off the lights,
let me see the sparks in your eyes.
Please, don't go any farther,
let me sail into your safe harbour.

Tell me that story again,
of the boy defeating a monster.
Love is always stronger than fear,
hold on to it dear.

Eric Shaw (12)

Through The Eyes Of A Ragdoll

First thing in the morning
When the sky is bright blue
I wake up in joy to see the sight of you
Your eyes are still shut, gentle and tight
You suddenly open them and I am your first sight
You see my face and slowly smile
Then you say, "I will play in a while"
You go get washed and then get dressed
Then you hug me and say
"This ragdoll's the best!"
You get the other teddies and play away
Then I think, this is a great day
You take me downstairs
All the way outside
Then you carefully put me
On the neon blue slide
You push me so gentle
The slide was so good
Then before I knew it
I was in the mud
I knew what this meant
I've been here before
You put me in water
With bubbles galore
So here I am sitting
Just covered in suds

This day will be fun
And we'll still be best buds.

Amy Jane Clewes (12)

Not Enough

You want me,
I can see it.
I like you,
Don't get me wrong.

However, there is this girl,
There always is.
I don't want you, but I do
I want her too.

Which one shall I pick?
I'm not too sure.
Let's just mess around with their hearts,
It will be entertaining for me and the boys.

The easy option is her,
Because she likes me.
I'll go with that one,
I'll lead her on.

I'll tell her I love her,
That I have changed.
I'll tell her that I want her,
That I need her.
When really all I want is a girlfriend.

I'll leave her on delivered,
I won't reply.
It will make her sad,

It will turn into a game, for me.
This is going to be entertaining.

It will make her broken-hearted,
Me and the boys get a good laugh out of it.
I can't wait.

Toxic relationships,
Happen every day for girls and boys.
No one deserves to be treated like this,
'Luck is when you love someone and they love you the same'.

Amelie Hunter (12)

Is This The End?

Suddenly I can see the smooth yet sharp texture of plastic resting against my tongue
The taste in my mouth is unusual and it is not a pleasant taste like my food
I can only see the crystal-clear water of the sea
But my eyes are struggling to stay open because I am terrified

My mind wanders back to a time when I was happy and carefree
I enjoyed swimming around with my fellow turtle friends
There were many of us and every day was an adventure
How I wish things were like they used to be

On the horizon I see someone swimming over
A sense of panic comes to me
The same thing that happened to me could happen to my friends
This could be the end…

Suddenly the feel of plastic disappears and I look up
I see a person who is very friendly and kind
After a few minutes, I feel much better
Now I know there is always hope in the world.

Sophie Edwards (12)

Through The Eyes Of Astra

Out in the night she neighed,
Seeking the lush grass under the frost and snow,
Where she had once grazed the wind howled.
The bare oak's branches bowed low
The tall pine trees scowled.

She shook her mane in fear
At the wolves' hungry cries.
Howling, howling, howling
The wolves hungrily howled at the dark night's sky.
The pack's despair was clear,
Their sorrowful wailing was near,
To the cold ears of Astra.

The wolves had scented her...
Their white fangs glistened in the ghostly moonlight,
As though they were snarling without a stir.
The mare's knees stiffened
And she galloped
Over the meadows...
Over the hills...
To the safety of the herd.

The wolves in vain
Weakly scampered back,
Howling, howling, howling
The wolves hungrily howled at the dark, starry sky.

Sofija Latinkic (11)

My Name Is...

My name is Martin Luther King Junior
I was strong, unique and I was black
People thought of me as a peculiar
But deep down inside I was sad

Sad that America was so racist
I knew that I had to do something
I made a speech, hopefully persuasive
What I wanted to say was that I had a dream

Where white people could treat us like the same
Where my children could actually grow up
Properly, just like the white people did
I wanted people to know my name

I wanted to see black people holding flags
I wanted to see them all feeling safe
I didn't want black people treated as slaves
I wanted all humans to feel so safe

I wanted us to be able to travel a bus
And not to be replaced with a white person
I knew eventually America will adjust
So that all people are created equal

Together we will stop discrimination
This nation will rise
Because together both races make a nation
A nation of joy, equality and excellence.

Isabelle Main

Anxiety's Darkest Attribute

Yet again, I have fallen a victim to my own pernicious thoughts.
Like the boiling blood that staggers through my body,
I supply myself with superstitions that gush through the anatomy of my brain,
Poisoning everything in sight.
It's as though I'd been thrown into a continuous summit of darkness,
With no end to hope for.
Alone and unconscious, with nothing but motionless theories to eat away at my sanity.
Incrementally, they crowd my mind.
A familiar murmur calls me closer. And closer.
Nor a human, nor an animal but a thing.
"Use me! Put an end this eternal trauma."
Not a single - not even the slightest - inkling of control over what life-daring action clenches my mortality at its fists.
Hidden behind my numb exterior,
A whirl of wind spirals around my head;
My brain recklessly squabbles with my limbs in a battle of confusion or certainty,
And my soul completely out of the mix.

Amber Igbo (15)

The Last Spark

There I was,
Fighting for my country,
Held at gunpoint,
Knowing I'm leaving my family.

Memories flooding back to me,
As the bullets pierce through the air,
My last minutes on this planet,
As I no longer care.

The bullets whistle,
As they fly through the sky,
Launching into my body,
Causing me to die.

As I float to Heaven,
My corpse on the ground,
Remembering those I have lost,
As my heart no longer pounds.

Flying up,
As I see my family huddle,
When all I really want to do,
Is just give them a cuddle.

Although I'm dead,
I died for my country,
I am distraught,
As my family look up glumly.

It's quiet up here,
As I'm all on my own,
But I died as a soldier,
And not as an unknown.

As my parents live on,
And my children get older,
I hope they remember,
That I was a great soldier.

I hope they all know,
That I didn't die in vain,
Can't wait for the time,
When we all meet again.

Ben Winchcombe (12)

Lost In Their Own Minds

You look at them
And wonder where they are
We see them
And hope that they can see us too
We love them
And hope that they still love us
We miss them
And wish they remembered who we are
We hug them
Hold them tight in the hope of no fight
We talk of common interests
Only to find they don't share them anymore
We cry
Only to wish they were still them
We hope that one day they will be the same
Knowing there is no cure
We ask about their day
Only to hear a lovely story
We yearn for the truth
With only fantasies and tales to be told
We wish to understand
But no test can give us that
We sit by their beds
For them to ask, are you the girl who does the laundry?
We hope for answers
We hope for change

We hope for things to be what they once were
But that will never happen
There is no cure
We can hope all we want for them to return
But in reality we can only hope to become a character in their fantasy.

Isabel Hall (17)

The Mirror On My Wall

Let me share a secret
Of what I really see
But you see this secret
It stays between you and me

I see her in the morning
Her hair is always a mess
She stares at me before yawning
Her brow furrowed with stress

I see her pose for pictures
Plastering on a smile
Her emotions are a mixture
I have not seen a genuine smile
In quite a while

I see her cry when she looks at me
Hands feeling over her skin
She looks as though she can't agree
And stares like what she can see is grim

I see her frowning at her phone
It never leaves her sight
I can see she still feels alone
Although she talks to her 'friends' all night

So if you haven't realised
I'm the mirror leaning on the wall

And if you haven't realised
I really see it all.

Taaliyah Parris-Sarrington (16)

The Holocaust - I Shall Never Die Forgotten

We played, we played, we were loved
We were ripped away from our future
Parents mourned as we went, yet it was their turn next
We were nothing more than children

We had a life, now not ours to keep
We had our dreams, now made to be nightmares
Hope was our saviour, soon there was no such thing
The night was as bright as the morning tomorrow
Our cattle will rule the town of silence
For we shall not die forgotten, yet our sins will

Morning came and all was light, not for long
I despised the moment where I would see only the back of my eyelids, yet soon was the time
My knees collapsed in the mud before me
And all feelings shattered like glass
As the robin flew before me, it had stared or glared, you could not tell which
Like all birds, its trust burnt like wood as I reached out to its attractive wings, it flew away
Guns were raised, but as long as the robin flies, I will never die forgotten.

Dylan Ridley (12)

A Normal Day

Imagine feeling suffocated in your own home
Can you ever remember feeling so alone?
School's online and family facetimes
In our gardens trying to get tan lines.

The radio is almost always on
People saying this is a government con,
It's just blurry voices ringing in my ear
While we are waiting for news we actually want to hear.

The nurses who fight to save our lives
For every one they save, another one dies,
Showing the population much-needed guidance,
Brave or unlucky I haven't decided.

"I miss you!" are words I hear more and more
"I miss when you used to show up at my door.
I can't wait until we can have just a normal day
I know you can't, but I wish you could stay."

Maybe this all happened for a reason
This is a change, a brand-new season,
The Earth's seas are bluer and the grass is greener
People are happier and the air is cleaner.

Aimee Grace Heaney-McKee (15)

The Need For Change

I dream of freedom and a world of acceptance,
but of that I wait with no expectance.
I have learnt the hard way that life is unfair,
it is just something that I have learnt to bear.
I am hated for who I am,
as if my appearance makes me less of a man.
I walk into the room for the first time,
and it is as if I have committed a crime.
Trust is hard to earn and friends hard to make,
it is a good thing that my spirit is hard to break.
The injustice fills me with sorrow,
but I know that I must live for tomorrow.
I hope that my life will improve.
I do not wish to be pitied, hated or judged,
all I want is a chance.
A chance to prove,
that I am not evil or weird,
just different but not to be feared.
So the next time you look down on someone like me,
Think of this poem and just leave them be.

Rosabella Rajack (16)

A Dog's Point Of View In Lockdown

What is happening in the world today?
My humans are staying home all day.
Not going to work, no going to school,
It seems that staying home is now the new rule.

Everyone insisting on taking me for a walk,
It's times like this, I wish I could talk.
Apparently exercise will keep them sane,
But if I'm honest it's now becoming a pain.

Always in my way, the house is a mess,
And it's not just the house I must confess.
I'm sure my mum doesn't even brush her hair,
And she really doesn't even seem to care!

Pyjamas are worn all day and night,
The kids are going crazy and just seem to fight.
Their boredom is really starting to kick in,
But they need to obey in order to win.

We need to beat this virus I have heard,
The damage it's causing is just absurd.
As much as I want the house back to myself,
I also want everyone to be in good health.

Leah-Rose Manning (14)

Just Like You!

I have autism.
Story of my life:
Our mouths are knives.
You use yours the wrong way, you get danger and violence back from mine. Use it the right way. Helpful and caring I will be!

I have autism.
I'm a fire alarm.
Trigger me,
You will hear my sirens crying for help

I have autism.
My heart is a bone,
You shatter it with your hurtful words.
It takes a long time for it to recover.

I have autism.
My eyes are ice skates,
Slipping out of control, but I understand!

I have autism.
My head is in the clouds!
Dreaming in my fantasy
When reality is a struggle.
I am really just like you!
The times when I'm being bad.
I'm not trying to make you mad.

I want to make you proud.
Can't you see how hard I try?

I can do all the things that you can do,
I just need a bit more time!
Learn to love me for who I am and best friends we'll be.

Maisy-Ilar Moazzenkivi

In The Belly Of The Sea

Waves flowing in and out,
Wafting, drifting all about,
Encompassed by an illimitable sapphire sea,
How more monotonous could this be?

A fire opal is scorching my head,
And aquamarine is chilling me to the bone!
Oh do I miss my nice, comfy bed,
Instead I have to sleep on frothy sea foam.

Surrounded by water for miles on end,
On my body seasickness has been inflicted,
There is nowhere to run and nowhere to bend,
I am stuck stiff and held hostage by this liquid,

It is like ample amount of money is available to me,
But I can't spend any of it,
Like that I have an abundance of water which is available and free,
But I can not drink a single bit,

Patiently waiting day by day,
I don't know how much longer my patience can stay,
I cannot wait here from April to May,
I have a will so there must be a way.

Oh! In the distance I see a bay,
Soon help will be on its way.

Zaeem Karnachi (11)

NHS

There was a part to be played,
a shape to be filled,
and they rose to the challenge...

They stand at the end of the empty aisle at where there is no food left on the shelves,
They hide their tears as they walk home hungry and tired,
And sit to mourn the patients whose hands they held while they died in the short time they had between shifts,
and they are still wondering,
why they rose to the challenge...

Watching the patients slowly leave this world their hearts wrench,
Daily,
they watch them suffer,
alone,
they wipe the tears from their eye as they listen to the ones with no family to talk to before they pass away,
and they are still wondering,
why they rose to the challenge...

When they cry,
it's not painless,
the salt from their tears stings their face
Sores from the protection that marks,
and they are still wondering,
why they rose to the challenge...

Jessica Douglas (12)

Cutting Strings

You know you've stepped out of childhood
when you can no longer pinpoint your best friend's house
from their street.

The same house that you went to
every Tuesday for hot dogs,
the one that you learnt to make a fort
and whispered innocent secrets beneath the sheets.

You know they're not the same person anymore
- or rather, you're not - when you merely say hello
when you pass on the streets,
despite constantly reminiscing
in the comments section of our old favourite bands.

That's not to say I don't love them anymore.
I do.
I still cherish every moment I spent on the fields,
each of us laughing under the violet skies
before the night called us home.

We still sleep under the same sky,
but a few inches more apart.
And that's okay,
because the world keeps on spiralling
and cutting strings is the only way to keep moving.

Megan Frost (18)

Duffy The Dog's Lockdown

My owners are home,
They never leave me,
They are here when I wake up,
They are here when I go to sleep.

The smelly one seems more stressed lately - I don't know why!
I'm happier than ever playing fetch,
Having more scratchy, scratchy, belly rubs,
And having an extra-long walk every day.

Why would they be unhappy?

They are a bit mean to me though,
No more Daycare, what have I done?
On my walks I can't run off, which makes it a lot harder to smell everything,
I can't go near my other doggy friends either,
I'm starting to wonder why they don't let anyone in or out the door,
Or why my mum is getting more stressed by the day.
I love snuggling up to them at night, when they are watching the talking photo.

Even though I like my family
I miss other dogs,
I hope I can see them soon.
When will my life go back to normal?

George Ludlow (18)

The Heartbeat Of The Nation

Minutes, seconds - its heart does not stop,
Pumping out the blood of selfless staff coming through,
Seeping into capillaries to help people feeling askew,
Lub dub, lub dub
"Hello, how can I help you?"

Pulse racing, it's tachycardiac,
The persevering paramedics, dedicated doctors and noble nurses,
Work late on night shifts even when their entire body aches,
Lub dub, lub dub
"I'm so sorry about the wait."

Something has happened.
Embolism? Stroke? Heart attack?
No matter, it will be here, so never fear!
Lub dub, lub dub,
"Hand me my protective gear."

Overworked, overwhelmed,
But beat after beat,
Its circulatory system continues to meet,
The never-ending demands and is a
Helping hand,
Saving multiple lives across the land.

Thank you to the National Health Service, the heartbeat of the nation.

Sakeena Rajpal (17)

Through Their Eyes

Smiles emitting from a youthful face
Laughter emerges in an enlightening way,
So happy and full of life they say
They all but her see it that way.

To them her hop to her step is joy,
To them her stories are tales of toys,
To them her imagination is wild,
To them her wondering is a time-waster worthwhile.

The truth lies beneath it all
The reasons, the story, the tales she talks,
The riddles intertwined within her words
The meaningful meaningless is how she works.

The smiles are liars, living masks,
Laughter a comforter hiding the dark,
Her hope brings pain, her body saw,
Her wondering is her trying to hide from it all.

Through their eyes is a different story
Through her eyes is a life and reality where nobody is sorry,
So judge you may but be assured
You may have her story half-finished and oh so wrong.

Chloe Dark (16)

Wildfire

I looked up from the floor,
I went to climb a tree.
I wanted to explore,
My friend disagreed.

When I went to climb it was very hot,
The tree suddenly caught fire.
So I could not.
It turned into a wildfire.

I tried to get my friend away,
But he thought we were playing games.
So he ran far away,
He didn't come back out of the flames.

It was unbearable,
I saw blue lights flash.
It was unstoppable,
My fur was covered in ash.

Firefighters arrived,
They were searching for trapped things.
They found me and made me surprised,
That's when the battle begins.

They wrapped me in a blanket,
But couldn't keep the fire under control.
The flames were gigantic,
They could not be controlled.

I got checked out,
I got given eucalyptus, which I ate.
I then heard that the fires were finally out,
My friend could have been saved!

Ele Pike (14)

Maya Angelou

I have had a sad beginning and a low time
I found happiness in grooving and moving with my fly
I let things flow to only lead to a disaster
Life carried on with a new leaf for me to master
I mastered it well to receive gratitude and praise
I became known as a great leader for my attitude and ways
I speak through poetry
I speak through my heart
I speak with words so clear they would pierce through your heart
In hard times I never give up to show that I rise
I have always thrived
I've always shone
I have a passionate style and compassionate words
Please don't see me as self-centred, but your guide
Use the words I speak
Use my actions
To show the world how to live
To show yourself how to be
I stay standing in the darkest times
For I am a light that cannot be broken easily
For I am Maya Angelou.

Melody Wright (13)

The Wave Of The Night

April fifteenth, Nineteen twelve.
Over two thousand souls on board.
One hundred and sixty minutes.
So many safety measures ignored.

Over two thousand souls on board.
Water slowly trickled into each room.
So many safety measures ignored.
The air laden with gloom.

Water slowly trickled into each room.
Sixty-five souls, each lifeboat could hold.
The air laden with gloom.
Only twenty-eight were on the first boat, drifting into the cold.

Sixty-five souls, each lifeboat could hold.
Here I stand, Wallace Hartley am I.
Only twenty-eight were on the first boat, drifting into the cold.
Strumming my violin, with my head held high.

Here I stand, Wallace Hartley am I.
One hundred and sixty minutes.
Strumming my violin, with my head held high.
April fifteenth, Nineteen twelve.

Megan Powell (12)

Chernobyl Fire

C hernobyl, a huge disaster in history
H ere with the ones who have deceased is a mystery
E rratic, it was very, all of the area, cut
R adiation levels zooming up and up but
N othing this bad happened in such a long time
O f all the families that had lost a loved one in the explosion, in dismay
B ut this is the reality
Y es, things like this that happen, it's insanity
L ost in the world without their loved ones!

F or all that have died, whether animal or human
I t will never be the same, all of them in ruins
R emember this moment as a tragedy for Ukraine
E ventually it got put out, but it will never be forgotten.

Robert James Tibulca (11)

Save Me

When I was born the world was big
I grew tall, big and strong
I provided oxygen through my leaves
For all of your special needs

One morning I awoke
To see one of my friends deceased
I was confused and angry
For it was taken by the beast

As the day passed by
Some trees had to say goodbye
But I am still here trying not to live in fear

But one night I awoke
To see a hill of trees in smoke
I tried to breathe but it was too late
It was not the time to hesitate

My roots wanted to be from the ground
But I was a tree so I couldn't walk around
I was scared, I wanted to scream
But nothing would come out of me
The beast had got a hold of me.

Sherise Amanda Hudlin (11)

What Lurks In The Dark

It came one night,
In the deepest, darkest shadows
Stalking all who never dare to sleep.

It came with razor-sharp claws
Ready to slice a suit of armour in one strike
And a pair of colossal, jet-black wings
Which could blow away anything in its path with the slightest movement.
Its horns emerged in the dead of night
Longing to show anyone its monstrosity.

It came for my friend,
Waiting, waiting outside of her bedroom window
The blinds were shut but she couldn't help herself
For just a little, minuscule peek.

It burst that night into a flurry of rage and evil
Grasping my friend with an iron grip,
And its grotesque teeth,
Yearning for a sumptuous dinner
That was the end of her, gone, disappeared
But the beast wasn't over yet
No, no, not yet.

Maya Bazarnicka (11)

Curtains Drawn

Curtains drawn
Shrouding the room in darkness;
Darkness like the void I feel immensely
That void that stops me from loving her.

Curtains drawn
Masking her features as she lies in the crib.
The features that I wish so dearly to love
And the crib built in the happier days.

Curtains drawn
Hiding me from her
Like the games of peekaboo every child seems to love
As if they believe their mother has gone away

Maybe this time her mother truly has gone away
Taken by the suffocating thoughts I feel endlessly
Unable to touch her for the fear she may feel the emptiness too
The fear that I could corrupt her innocence with my poison

So I keep the curtains drawn
Away from the world's judgement
Away from my husband's concern
And away from her.

Cerys Rawlinson (15)

The Veteran

I close my eyes, as tightly as I can.
Just the memory, the distant, faint chants of a life left behind.

A fleeting glimpse is all I want, all I need
But I am drawn back to my reality as every hour, minute, second passes by,
Waving a last goodbye with an outstretched arm.
I can almost reach it, just inches away.

But I can't.

Though screwed eyes,
I can see it now,
The horror,
The pain,
Torment,
Pure evil.

I can't handle it,
I can't cope with it,
But I'm remembering it,
All of it,
With the grizzly parts left in.

No.
Please stop this,
I just want to forget.
To forget everything,

Forever.

A single tear sears down my withered cheek.

How can I blame them,
Any of them?
After all,

A monster is never born, it's made.

Alfie Williams (13)

Lost

It was once a wonder you know. Home. Mind.
It was long before you were even born.
In a palace of a thousand trees, it was a drop of gold in a sea of smaragdine.
And we were lost, enchanted, in this kind
utopian paradise, where enshrined
lies God's lush, tranquil garden, where adorned
by the Amazon's gift - the troubadour
of life - the sounds of rain on trees and hoots of birds are frozen in time.
My heart's still there - though we left long ago.
Amid the crowded city's din, we can
still feel the withering wind as it blows
and bellows smoke and chars and sears our skin.
We stare, eyes stinging, skin singeing and qualm
remembering nature: our fire-flooded home.

Prabhas Vedagiri (16)

The Real Heroes

Heroes are people who are make-believe
They live in places where no one sees
Special powers separate them from us
Breathing fire, magic, hocus-pocus stuff

Now in life these heroes are no more
We now see before us who we should really adore

The NHS have come together from far and wide
Making everyone open their eyes
For no longer does a hero wear a cape
But an apron and a mask with no escape

For these heroes lay down their lives
Giving us hope and keeping us alive

Keep climbing those mountains or a hill at a time
They show us the way to keep us alive
Forever in your debt, true heroes you are
May God keep you in his prayers; near and far.

Tegan Markey (12)

The Abyss

I am standing at the border to safety.
My heart is slowly drowning in fear.
Screams torture the void around me.

Lost homes.
Lost families.
Lost lives.

Fear.

I fall on the ground and stare
At the blue sky above that we all share:
How can you judge me if I am already less than human to you?

Funny. You do not remember.

We once have been part of the same unsteady stars,
The same ancient iron dances in our blood,
And we will turn into the same ashes someday.

We were the bright dots in the universe,
And now you are putting the last one in my book.
We adrift in the inky darkness.

I am scared of the dark.

But when I see the tears sparkling in the moonlight,
I hope they will flood the hearts with love
Again.

Wiktoria Maszorek

Image

"You're so fat, ugly and such a nerd!"
These are all things teens have heard.
"You're so annoying and have such big ears!"
All these things bring them to tears.

"Go away, no one likes you!"
They are all words they can't be true.
But they hurt, they ruin, they bring teens down to their knees,
As they are running from all this torture they don't leave behind any tease.

From everyone judging way too quick,
All they are doing is taking the mick.

Every word you say makes an impact,
Everything you say and how you act.
One slight word can cause devastation,
And that's just how you lose concentration.
You wonder why their grades are slipping,
It's just not worth it to give us a whipping.

Sophie Mulvenna (13)

Just Because...

Just because I might be different to you,
it does not mean you can make fun of me for being who I am.

Just because I might be different to you,
it does not mean that wearing glasses is bad - they helped with the fire.

Just because I might be different to you,
it doesn't mean you can ignore me,
I could have run the island my aunt's way.

Just because I might be different to you,
it does not mean I can be treated like a last-minute resource because I've got asthma and I am overweight.

Just because I might be different to you,
Can't I just have one chance?

Just because I might be different to you,
Wait. Isn't everyone different?
Isn't that why we are all so unique and special in our own little way?

Mia Patton (14)

Children Are Your Plants

At first,
You were mesmerised by the earthly glow,
The mellow dance of light that played upon my leaves ensnared you.
You were gripped at every movement.
Consciously
I watched you fill up with saturated holy water,
As you smiled upon my daily growth.
So I bestowed you with my godly fruits.
However,
You rejected my gifts.
And now
Your fugacious admiration has forsaken you.
My dry leaves stand as evidence
And these passing nights where my roots strangle me
Exhibit your sudden disinterest.
Without my beauty standing in your background
I will be thrown away.
Forgotten and replaced.
Your neglectfulness has set my future.

Amelia McEleavey (15)

The Interview

Did I get the job?
My nerves are off the scale,
Will I get good results,
Or will it be a fail?

Am I good enough for this place?
The question runs through my mind,
Is it the man in front that can beat me,
Or is it the woman behind?

All the intense training,
For the job I like,
I hope that they accept me,
And see someone they like.

The interviewers asked lots of questions,
They tried to put me off,
I wasn't going to waste any time,
With a stutter or a cough.

They tried to get to me,
Break my confidence,
But thankfully it didn't work,
As I showed resilience.

I was too busy focusing on the interview,
I'm not sure if I turned heads,
Am I good enough for the job?
The job of selling beds!

Ewan Collier (12)

Pollution

The phenomenal world is being shadowed by dark smoke
The pollution of sapphire seas and cutting down of towering trees
I can see heavenly scenery, a thing from the past
I can see the terrific tragedy.

The plastic, paper, all sorts of dreadful litter
The vast sea packed with toxic trash
I can see the pitiful animals' destruction
I can see the withering world.

The sickening pollution is harmful
The venomous poison pierces the innocent hearts.
I can see exhausts polluting the fresh air from industries
I can see the eventful end.

The lively world can change
The sensational sky, magical trees, and harmonic wildlife
I can see Earth as a beautiful, bountiful home to many
I can see a magnificent miracle.

Athviga Saththiyanthiran (12)

The Faceless Identity Of A Heavy Burden

The emptiness inside,
the numbness and the pain.
You're holding on so tightly,
to that ever-binding chain.

These voices are so loud,
everywhere just aches.
You're anyone but you,
maybe you're just a fake.

How do we move on?
when we look through rose-tinted glasses,
The memory stays permanent
after it's crumbled into ashes.

The silence is deafening,
the walls are closing in.
You're driven to the chasm,
your patience wearing thin.

All hope is slowly fading
yet there are still glimmers of light,
you must keep on pushing
and carry on the fight.

People can and do change,
this suffering isn't forever,

don't give up so easily
never say never.

Bailey Evatt (17)

The Furless Polar Bear

In the frozen arctic land, I roam,
Walruses and seals share the joy,
God has created this luxurious place of tranquillity,
Surrounded by the superb scenery,
He gave me shaggy, thick, wonderful fur,
The chills wouldn't kill me,
Something else atrocious would happen you'll see,
However, there is nowhere I could possibly flee,
I was once glad to have this home with all the necessities to survive,
But now climate change is occurring,
You have to concur,
I'm holding on to every strand of life I definitely don't prefer,
Whoever did this just neglects,
Would you like to know why I am furless?
Humans made me so...

Iman Mahmood (13)

Frantic Feelings

Walking down the crowded corridors
Feeling lonely and blue
No one looks up at you
Sitting at the back of class no one notices you
Whilst everyone has someone to talk to
Teachers don't make an effort and just leave you
Even when you have a mental health issue
You want to be noticed
But it's hard to be recognised

My heart's beating outside my chest
My hands continuously shaking as time is passing
But in my dreams, I am constantly running
Friends always texting me but don't understand how I feel
I want to tell someone, but I haven't got the courage like other people
As they have it easy and simple
The fear of me drowning and no one noticing
This was just the beginning...

Prachi Patel (14)

Through The Eyes Of A Homeless Soul

P is for poor. You are looked down on and worth nothing to passers-by.
O is for overwhelmed. You find yourself in a state that you cannot move a muscle because you are so exhausted.
V is for vacancy. People pass by thinking that you do not understand a thing and look down at you like a piece of dirt.
E is for exiled. Abandoned. When you cannot support yourself, no one comes to support you.
R is for regrets. You just wish that you could go back in time and fix everything.
T is for touring. Like a gypsy you just go wherever fate takes you.
Y is for yearn. All you have left do is to just yearn. Yearn for hope...

Faith Gebre (13)

Life As An NHS Worker In 2020

C aring for people with this illness is what I do
O riginally started in China but now is worldwide too
R unning around all day is what I do to save lives
O ptimistic, we all are hoping the death toll takes a dive
N ot everyone believes in this illness, I don't know how they can't
A ntidote we hope we can use to control the spread
V iolent this is, we should try and stay positive
I t's classed as a pandemic which is worse than a war
R uining people's lives is what this is doing
U ngratefully we were now hopeful for the new beginning
S ave yourself and don't go out, it helps the NHS!

Brooke Peto (11)

Euphoria

Blade down her throat;
god, those nails are long
long and pointy
long and pointy and smothered in her blood.
The police will believe it's a suicide
...
right?

Blade in my pocket;
the midnight air is crisp and tight.
Tight like a hug.
Tight like a hug? No -
I am being strangled.
Strangled for my sins.
But I am not a sinner; I am
simply just
a normal girl who
gets mad
sometimes.

Blade on the counter;
by the window, I felt safe.
One puff, two puffs;
god, I hate this city.
But by the window,
I felt safe.

I'm safe here, in this haven;
no one can hurt me, judge me or need me because
it's just me myself and I in this
euphoria.

Sabrina Mohammad (14)

A Kid's View Of Coronavirus On Lockdown

My life was fun and exciting
But I must admit that there are things that need changing
Schoolwork is draining
My siblings are annoying
And my parents are always complaining
It goes without saying
I do not miss school, but quarantine is boring
I've played every game, watched every film, when will this be ending?
The government is saying that lockdown will be extending
The NHS staff and key workers are doing amazing
But the amount of cases is increasing
All the deaths from this virus is frightening
And it is becoming slightly concerning
With it being scary all we can do is just keep praying
Stay at home, protect the NHS and save lives as Boris keeps saying.

Bruk Alemshet (12)

Isolation

This is our new normal staying indoors and doing our work
We have no need to rush, now that's a perk
We find ways to have fun
By making hot cross buns
It's not that fun in isolation
But we can pretend our sisters are at a coronation
We try to have fun in a different way each day
Since our friends are far, far away
Our nights are restless because we're scared
About this virus and how we weren't prepared
Our parents cut our hair
For a price that is fair
To be good and stay calm
Whist we grow our own farm
In the end we will be sad
But when it's all over we won't be mad
But all hope is not lost
When once again our paths will cross.

Daniel Laws

The Evacuee

Mum, will we die?
Mum, will we survive?
Mum, will we burn?
Mum, will we laugh?

I am being evacuated
I will say goodbye but won't return
I will go with a change of clothes in a dirty rag
And a flask filled with water and the tears down my cheeks

Mum said you will be back home soon
But it seems like forever and ever
I try to be brave but feel so alone

I don't know when I will come back
But when I do I know there will be shooting
But for now the air raids still happen
The houses still fall
And the people still die
Is there any hope for us all...?

Axel Bas Davies

I See Them, Through My Eyes, I See Them

He is begging for mercy,
he wants freedom,
but I will give him doom.
The mirror was reflecting his feelings through my left eye,
he had forced me to trap him there.
If he stayed with me this wouldn't have happened.
He lied.
He cheated.
He slept with her.
I hate her.
I hate him.
I hate them.
Worst is we came from the same parents,
I actually cared about her,
we laughed,
we played,
we told each other everything.
Why did she not tell me of him and her?
Was it fear?
I see her, through my right eye, I see her.
She is suffering.
Their expressions reflected their feelings,
they rest in peace under their graves.
I see them, through my eyes, I see them.

Juliet Gyan (15)

One Crisis, Two Different Worlds

Through the eyes, eyes on the freeing prize.
Is lockdown our saviour or breakdown?
A hard time for us was the famed COVID-19 virus.
2019 December thirty-first came the virus, one of the worst.
A point from every human eye, they couldn't sail, they couldn't fly.
Alaska to New Zealand, every country fell to its knees, all locked in an economy freeze.
On another hand, what about the land? The forests so grand and the beaches of sand?
Recovering from her crisis and reclaiming her lost territories.
The air is cleaner than before as Mother Nature is back in law.
Now, as the pandemic unfurls, we must hope for the best of both of these worlds.

Brandon Ellis (13)

Bright Future

The future is bright,
You will feel happiness the size of the sun,
All of the rain clouds of negativity will fade and you are going to be so happy,
There will be reasons to smile and laugh and live,
With all your hard work and determination over the years will pay off,
Those who didn't believe in you will be proven wrong,
You will walk in to tomorrow with confidence,
You will work so hard to be noticed and appreciated,
You will make the most of your life by living it,
There will be many people to share memories with,
So make the most of it
And live the life you have been blessed with
As the gift of life is the most valuable gift there is.

Alexander Rate (13)

There's No Place Like Home?

I'm trapped in a room paralysed with fear
Instead of water blood fills my tear
I can't leave because it's against the law
But nobody understands how I will suffer for evermore
It's okay for people who can stay in lockdown happily
But they don't come from a broken-down family
I'm trapped at home with all my freedom taken
Feel all alone, totally forsaken
Happiness for me is non-existent
Nothing has happened although my fighting is persistent
I'm ready within for you to hear my voice
But the terror inside gave me no choice
I'm trapped in a room paralysed with fear
But this time my blood loss is way too severe.

Ruqaya Bint Aslam (11)

Words Can Hurt

She was as pale as a ghost,
I could see the tears rolling down her cheek.
She was completely broken and lost

The hateful words rang through her head,
I could feel her hate.
For she wished she was dead.

She had cuts up her arms.
As people don't know when to stop,
I could see the blood running down her palms.

Every day the words linger,
Every day she hurt,
Every day the words hurt.

She was just a girl.
She had no one to help her,
She was a bullied schoolgirl.

She was permanently on alert.
Drowning in all the horrible words,
When will people learn that words can hurt?

Natalie Stocker

Death Row

Took only one act of madness
To lead to many slow, painful years
Trapped inside this concrete hell
Left there, helpless
Only three days left until this all will be over

Sleepless nights
Instant reactions
Constantly thinking about what life could have been like
And how differently I could have spent it
Only two days left until it will be all over

Engaged by steel bars
Spending my last few days staring at cold stone walls
With nights full of misery
All there is left to do is wait and wait
Only one day left until it will be all over.

Amber McIntosh

Stars In The Day

Look in the mirror, what do you see?
A girl standing there full of hopes and dreams
A future bright, what will she be?
Gorgeous eyes and a smile that beams

Look closer and you'll see her scars
Abuse in her past she will never tell
Her secrets hidden during the day like stars
At night they'll come and well -

Devour her whole, she is trapped and encaged
She will never escape from deep in her brain
Demons in her mind, a war is waged
She smiles, no one sees the pain

Internal struggle and internal war
Internal conflict in each and every mind
Almost each and every soul is tore
Be a friend and be more kind.

Scarlet Barras (17)

Locked In My Own World

Locked in my own world
Staring at the same four walls
All I can do is think of all the things I can't do.
My head is stuck like a fish in a net.
I long to see family and friends, to feel their gentle touch and the warmth of the sunshine in their smiles.
My legs feel as heavy as a bag of sand, I move around with the energy and vitality of a slow, sloppy sloth.
Anxiously, nervously I wait for this invisible killer to vacate our lives.
Too many lives have been taken too soon.
We should never forget our brave, fearless, courageous, guardians in masks, gloves and gowns; heroes we cheer, heroes we cheer.

Max Lavin (12)

The Fallen Star

A midnight-black, dusky sky,
Of sparkling glitter and distant cries,
A cavern of secrets and stories untold.
Mountains of treasure - hunters behold.

Across the ebony feathers of night,
There sparkled a magical, golden sight.
The milky speckles twinkled and twirled,
Soaring like diamonds across our world.

Like scattered emeralds of dying fire:
A beautiful blanket - there to admire.
Tales of great angels, dragons and war.
Screaming and lonely, loud as a roar!

Hold your breath; close your eyes,
Follow its light to the sunrise,
Once it's gone - oh star so soft,
Make a good wish - fingers crossed.

Lily Healey (13)

She

She whistles and sings, never complaining
As her hands become raw
From cleaning all our things.
She looks after us and puts herself last
Always making sure we are safe
And never making a fuss.
Not only a mother, a woman
Not only a woman, an inspiration
Not only an inspiration, an unsung hero.
She lays down in bed, tired and sore
But a smile on her face, because she loves us all.
She would give her life up for her children
And her life is made for them now
How she ever manages,
We can only dream how.
To the mothers from every place
We thank you for teaching us how to love
By giving your warm embrace.

Kayla Vicente (17)

Heart

He hurls his words like grenades.
They explode against us; each one is larger
than the last and we cower
in pain and despair.
I beat harder and harder, until I race so fast, I fear
I will explode myself.
But I do not get a chance.
He throws his final words and breaks
me first.
Her hands fly to me and press against the barrier
between us.
Desperately trying to hold me
together even as I
shatter.
Sparks fly from his heel as he turns and leaves.
At the slam of the door we crumple
to the floor.
She releases me to wipe her tears and I fall apart.
The pieces of me scatter the ground like
ashes.

Erika Lang (16)

This Must Stop

Playing and entertaining thousands every game
Abuse and racism heading towards his name
Sent out to do his job and given stick
2020 and it's still around but it should disappear in a flick
Must be horrible going home after an offence
But he keeps on going, it doesn't make any sense
It teaches him to be a better person and he has learnt so much
Over someone's skin colour, this should not be a fuss
Abuse given by his own nation, his own country, his own fans. This must end!
They must be punished, nothing less than a lifetime ban.

Max Alner (13)

A Lesson Learned

Gone, gone, gone from the Earth,
Mother Nature our creator,
Fighting back,
I don't blame her.

Years and years of abuse and suffering,
There comes a time we needed discovering,
Discovering our mistakes,
Discovering our damage,
Discovering our future before the world runs empty.

The balance of nature,
Once pure and innocent,
Now filled with pollution,
Wars and confusion.

Quickly, quickly how things become memories,
Of good times before,
Of bad times instore.

We need to embrace,
It's us who can change,
The survival of the planet,
For generations to flourish.

Laith Bixby (12)

Fight

Taking punch after punch
Having to block after block
He keeps sinking and sinking
I know I will break and break
But like the famous words said
You just can't beat the person who won't give up
So I realise he is getting tired
I see he is down to the wire
I see it is my time to strike
I punch him multiple times in the torso
I see he is regenerating strength
I know I have one shot
And I am going to make it count
I send a punch to his face
He woke up several minutes later
He realised he had lost.

Jayden Bianchina (12)

Damaged Goods

As I lay alone in the dark
Listening to the world come to a halt
I can't help but ask
Could it have been my fault?

The moonlight streaks through the blinds
Symbolic of the ray of hope that got me through
As I reach for closure there's just one answer I cannot find
What did I do?

Even Lucifer was once an angel
You mustn't judge at first glance
What appears evil might just be unstable
Could the cure be a second chance?

But as the sun intrudes its way into my silence
Realisation hits me at the core
I am a survivor of domestic violence
And I am a victim no more.

Kayleigh (15)

The Underdog

Underdog, outcast of society;
When at the bottom, there is no way up.
Fighting for the scraps of those above me,
Whose mess I am always forced to clean up.

Powerless in the face of injustice,
We are told to stay back and stay quiet.
And when we don't, when we find our purpose,
We are punished for causing a 'riot'.

But most tragic is not physical pain
But the corruption of the innocent,
Whose souls are blackened by the tainted rain,
Who are forsaken to years of torment.

We are the underdogs; left abandoned.
But with the truth of life, we are burdened.

Farah Khalif (17)

The Invisible Energy

What keeps you alive?
I bet you don't think it's me.
It will be love or faith that makes you survive.
I can guarantee.

What keeps you alive?
It won't be your lung.
But you don't mind when I thrive.
I've been here since you were young.

What keeps you alive?
Don't mind me.
You can continue to strive,
Cutting down that tree.

What keeps you alive?
Open your eyes.
Without me you wouldn't be alive.
I am your supplies.

I keep you alive.
And if you disrespect me.
Contaminate me.
Destroy me.

Then -
I hope your love and faith have strength.

Grayce Kimberley (15)

Pressure

The words spinning around my head,
Too quiet, too loud, too thin, too fat,
"Just be like us!" that's what they said.

Are they real or fake?
Only they know,
I let their words overtake.

The screaming in my ears,
"Don't wear that, it's disgusting"
It almost brought me to tears.

My brain gradually becoming more dark,
Voices threatening me,
It was like my thoughts were being eaten by a shark.

I couldn't take the pressure anymore,
The blade stealing blood from my hand,
I scraped it down my chest and my skin tore...

Talia Martin (13)

Batman

I stood in Crime Alley
After he ran from the kill
Both my parents shot dead
By a man named Joe Chill

This ended an era
Blew out a candle
But opened some doors
Only I could go handle

I created the Bat
A man of such strength
A man to be feared
To keep convicts at length

Gotham is better
But not good enough
Crime is still lurking
But still I stay tough

I am the Bat
Ready to fight
Convicts beware
My hits won't be light!

Aaron Speak

Puzzle Are Fun

Life is a puzzle
Sometimes it's tough
Sometimes it's simple
Sometimes you find your way
Other times you simply lose your way
But every time it's fun I say
This puzzle has to be solved
Everyone has to play
Because life is a puzzle I say

Of wildlife or a bread knife
Puzzles are my life
About the sun or someone's loved one
Puzzles are fun

Puzzles don't give us troubles
Puzzles can work miracles
Come on let's go on an adventure
So we can find some treasure
Let's do a puzzle, everyone, because
Puzzles are fun

Ruqqiya Shahid

Coronavirus

From a bug to a pandemic
The worst you will ever see
From life to death
Worst in history
No funeral, no love, not even a goodbye
Instead you watch them horribly die
The NHS workers working night and day
Oh God please keep this pandemic away
Watching your loved ones pass away
Watching them suffer is the worst I can say
No joy, no love, just misery
It is surely the worst in history
As they die we cry
From night to day
Oh, God, oh God
Keep this horror away!

Yusuf (11)

Man

Man.
Came first, now last.
Should be seen and not heard.
Your input is no longer valid.

Man.
March to die.
No choice is given.
Do your country proud.

Man.
Never gets a moment to breathe
"Just man up and deal with it."
Depression is mere exaggeration.

Man.
Impossible to do right.
Trash. Pigs. Scum.
All are these.

Man.
Beaten. Battered. Bruised.
It's okay. Doesn't matter.
"He deserved it."

Man.
Homo sapien.
Part of huMAN.
But barely treated like one.

Man.
Wanted, not.
Desired, not.
Needed?

Yes.

Jo-Andrea Mirembe (18)

Them

They say
So much we don't even know
If it's true.
They say
Lies, lies and more lies.
Trick and scare the people,
Fib, scam and con the people,
And you can control them.
Like they
Control us.
They say
"Hey, we don't know what you're talking about"
But we all know
That if you've told one lie
You must've told a thousand more
Because after all, why stop at two
When there's so many more?
They say
Nothing.
All we can say is
Exposure and humiliation
Will soon come your way
Just you wait
And see.

Hawwaa' Bint Mahmood (16)

Apollo

I gallop gracefully through the fields,
I look for grass all day.
She brings me in and to my stable, for a net of hay.
I love it when she brushes me,
My mane all smooth and straight.
I know that when she tacks me up,
It's going to be great.
We ride together all day long,
My girl upon my back.
I love to wander through the woods, upon a dusty track.
In dressage I dance gracefully,
Perfecting all the moves.
The judges watch me carefully, trotting with my hooves.
I am so lucky to be me,
I love my girl and she loves me.

Jessica Hughes

Cyborg

I've woken up in a lab
Certainly this is a hub
It's a bit of a blur
I hear the sounds which recur

The door has opened and, old man
He told me all that happened then:
"You died a hundred years ago
But now my friend you're free to go."

"I scanned and copied your brain
Almost unreal to explain."
Just now I start to understand
I am a Cyborg, not a man

I feel emotions, I can think
Connections are establishing
I'm checking files that were saved
My Cyborg mind starts to rave...

Anastasia Bobosco (13)

What A Sight

I can see bright laughter and the cool crisp breeze
As the summer sunlight gently embraces me.

I can see the comforting aroma of hot home-made meals.
I can see how the soft, new skin of my grandchild feels.

I can see barks and cries and shouts and whispers.
I can see your aching heart and your gentle whimpers.

I can see myself when the days were young and I was naive,
Believing every view and vision I carelessly perceived.

Is it not clear? Can't you see?
You don't need eyes to see like me.

Tara Olawoye (16)

The Broom

I have a thousand legs but can only lean,
You make me feel dirty so you can feel clean,
Woe is me whom you fill with dirt and grime,
And you can't be bothered to clean though you have the time,
You might dream I enjoy being used,
Well I'm sad to say I have bad news for you,
I find my purpose tiring,
And highly unrewarding,
The fruits of my labour are shrivelled, self-pitying and sour,
Until my very final hour,
When they are wrenched from me,
Then I am tossed away to lie into a pile of debris.

Eliza Khaliq (11)

The Fallen

On bloodstained land the bodies weep
Far from home
Of death they reek
They mark the place of soldier's brave
A long time ago
Their guns did crave
A victory for us

Inside a ditch another dies
What were sweet words
Now ugly lies
A bomb goes off
Now the norm
Men whisper soft
Words forlorn
A victory for them

Finally, the war is done
What were once homes
Are now all gone
In their graves the dead men rot
The dead men weep
For their sins won't be forgot
These foolish wars for what?

Gabriella Smith (13)

A Sunflower

I lie in a field,
Happy as can be,
Rays of sunlight gently kissing me,
Birds fly high in the sky,
Singing sweet tunes to the lovely sunny morning,
Spreading joy,
Black and yellow bees come and visit me,
In my field of sunflowers,
I am never lonely,
Overjoyed children skip and dance,
Sharing stories that make them laugh,
Falling onto the wet grass,
Taller and taller I will grow,
The more I grow,
More petals I show,
I lie in a field,
Happy as can be,
Rays of sunlight gently kissing me.

Shanice Steele-Henry (11)

The End

The exquisite planet is slowly coming to an end
Scorching, devastated and destroyed
It was tremendous and filled with lush growth.
Vivid, extraordinary and phenomenal.

The Aegean Sea, a graveyard
Melancholic, miserable and terrifying.
Coastal cities brimming with dark polluted water
Extinction, desolation, famine.

The glistening, sparkling snow, never seen again
Crunchy, cloudy and chalk-white
It annihilated the splendid, sensational polar bear.
Massacre, slaughter... the end.

Varnan Saththiyanthiran (14)

A Prisoner Of War

The cold truth of war
Which you could hardly believe,
The end is in sight
But I'm not ready to leave.

In these times it's hard
To speak my farewells,
My only true friend
I'll tell you my hells.

I've spent so much time here,
Trying not to feel the fear.
The darkness is coming, I can feel it all around,
I can hardly feel my body now,
Just lying on the ground.
I bid you farewell my friend and wish you the best.
I hope you get home my friend as well as the rest.

Brooke Gander (13)

All Of Us

I look at each human being, as if they were a flower
Some are weak, and some have power,
Some grow tall, some stay small,
Some who open up, and some who choose to keep shut
Some who blossom at an early age,
Some who bloom at a later stage,
Some so beautiful words can't define,
Some more on the side of the divine,
Some who try to grow to greater lengths
And some who stay with their born strengths
But no matter what we choose to claim
In the end we are all the same.

Libby Laredo (11)

The Great Things

I see you standing there
Right in front of me
I see you brush out your hair
Right before you sleep
I hear the things you say
Looking at yourself
I hear you every day
Comparing yourself
I see your tears
I feel your insecurities
I know what you think
I wish you could see the great things
The great things I see
When you stand in front of me
I am the mirror
And your reflection is what I see
I see all the great things
I hope one day you too will see
The great things.

Shania Miah

An Autumn Day

I stepped into the bright wood
And for a while I stood
Admiring what I could see before me
I felt completely free

Autumn leaves fell silently
Floating down almost lifelessly
I felt the gentle breeze
And almost fell to my knees

I could hardly see the floor
Because of the beautiful outdoors
The wood lit up with orange
The whole place felt amazingly adoring

I love this autumn day
And I don't want it to go away
But I know that too soon
Then will come the moon.

Imogen Reynolds (13)

The Bat

He doesn't change with his powers
He uplifts the country
The man is a genius yet we know who he is
We do not see his face
He looks at the people of the country, he stares
Using his watchful eye
He is the guardian
Some say God has sent him to protect them
Some say he is a freak
Some say he should be arrested for the crimes he has committed
The only way he could hurt the country is if he left
Who is he?

Joshua Lyon

The War

The wind screamed in our ears
Slicing our skin with the icy breeze
It was like being gradually split open by a knife
The guns weren't our enemy, the weather was.

Slowly traipsing across the trench
Realising that I was the only one alive
I knew it was the end, if the enemy didn't take me
The weather would.

This is my end
This is my story
And this is my short life as a 15-year-old boy.

Riley Lake (12)

Life In The Trenches

What lies ahead is all fun and games
It will only be for a few days
It will only be a playground fight
It won't even be a fright
What a shock
It didn't rock
Can't it end?
Can't we make amends?
Down there with mud
Covered in blood
Itching a head full of lice
And feeling rat bites
Out in the cold
Being bold
Having shots
With other Scots
Took a shot
That took some guts
But my gun was already pointing at my chest
I was already stressed.

Lola Swan (13)

Lost In Time

Lost is the person who was wrongly accused
abandoned by society who only refuse
to hear their sorrowful pleading
as they were left for dead, bleeding.

Rich is the person who committed the crime,
sending their partner to be lost in time
showering in gold and diamonds
their partner stuck on an island.

Forgotten will they forever be,
insanity has made others flee,
for they shall never grow up
they are alone,
lost in time.

Grace Winterton (14)

Time Is Life

Time is what we need
Time is what we are
How will we do without it?

Seconds go into minutes
... Minutes into days!
How can we not realise
How quick life fades away?

Birds singing in the trees
Whales playing in the sea
Waves dancing beautifully
What a delightful painting I wish it came to me!

Let's grab a dream in the night
and hold hands with the fight.
Hope flies high
Come... make sure the Earth doesn't die!

Bruno Correia

Corona

It is Corona,
It is very baaad
It will make you mad,
Gotta stay inside,
Ain't get to see the homies,
Just stayin' at home,
Ain't called being lazy,
She said, "When we free?" Hmm, hmm?
Government said two...
... Two what?
Two weeks, months or years?
Why is it sunny?
I just realised,
Corona is good for nature,
Stops humans,
Going out, harming the environment.
And this is the end
Of the song!

Ahmed Muhammad (11)

Coronavirus

In the news you have probably heard of the Coronavirus
Which means you cannot go on holiday to somewhere like Cyprus
Make sure you wash your hands every day
And stay inside to have a play
Try not to touch your face
Otherwise the virus will spread faster than a race
The NHS are taking care of us, they are our heroes
So let's save lives and get the amount of deaths to zero!

Neive Sarah Homewood (11)

Yellow

I'm standing long and strong with my braches stretching out tall,
I'm dancing in the wind, not a care at all.

I can hear the water trickling down the stream
And the birds singing their beautiful song.

I feel free, all my branches relaxed,
All my sad thoughts blown away.

I'm standing up and strong with my branches stretched out tall.
My leaves are changing colour my leaves are ready to fall.

Eva Doherty

TikTok Famous

I woke up today feeling amazing
When I went to the window, I stood gazing,
My sister came up screaming,
"Look at your phone it's beaming!"
"With what?"
"Look at the dot!"
"OMG! How is this possible?"
"Never think the impossible!" I yelled at the top of my voice
"I'm TikTok famous!"

Lois Ashfield (13)

Bonco The Water Dragon

You are blue
Blue as the sky
I see you flying above me

You are blue
Blue as the sea
So come fly with me

You are blue
Blue as the moon
That one that shines above me

You are blue
Blue as the flowers
The ones that people give to me

You are blue
Blue as the ice
You are the one who feeds me.

Maeva-Grace Arzur-Kean (13)

Memory Lane

As I stepped out unto the grassy plain
It was like taking a trip down memory lane
It was like a miracle
I felt like a captive that was set free
The fact of meeting my distant cousins made me feel so happy
Finally, it would feel like one big family
We would pray, then play all through the day
"Good times, good memories!" I would often say
As I took a trip down memory lane.

Ifesinachi Chinwuko (12)

Today

The paradox of life is to move,
move quickly,
move slowly,
move at your own pace.

You need to be content and relish the charm of the present,
so many people try to
grow up too quickly.
But all you need is
the happiness that will
come to stay.

They say,
the days are long,
but the years are short.
Today,
shouldn't be filled with
doubt and worry
but with
Innovation and destiny.

Lauren Carter (15)

Pigeons

We are hated
To steal we are fated
Bound to be shooed away
Bound to be dull and grey
We battle for all food
Our fates doomed

And yet beyond this torment lies
People with their food bags
That sit on park benches
Those who our hunger they quench
Those who are old, those who help
Those like us pigeons grey and black.

Nicholas Bors-Sterian (12)

How Did The Sky Look?

Hidden away on the bathroom floor
My breath broken and rapid
I try to find my purpose
But then I look up
And the window bleeds in moonlight
A dark sky with freckles of stars
My breath calms
And I admire flecks of celestial beauty
A view so powerful it can halt my thoughts
Maybe my purpose, like these stars
Is just to be.

Abbie Hooper

Saving

He made a decision,
He left his comfort
And journeyed all the way
In order to save.

He arrived at his destination
He met with hatred, hostility
And criticism all the way
In order to save

He used discussion
He diagnosed their ailments
And healed all the way
In order to save

He had determination
He loved undeniably
And worked all the way
In order to save.

Mofijinfoluwa Olayiwola (11)

The Prisoner Of War

I looked into the dark,
I realised it was night,
I heard a bark,
And I felt a bite.

I saw people get hurt,
I didn't want to speak,
They were treated like dirt,
And the war was at its peak.

The pain in my arm was too much to bear,
I knew I would shortly die,
If I didn't get medical care.
I painfully lay down and cry.

Honey Parkhouse

A Letter From COVID-19

From hand to hand I go,
I am really dangerous as you know.
So many have died and yet some don't care,
Until it's their time to start praying in despair.

The community has found unity,
Maybe it's time to give you another opportunity.
The longer I stay the more will die,
So, the time has come to say goodbye.

Kiara Campos Ribeiro

Rosa Parks

Even if you nudge,
I will not budge.
I cannot move,
Instead society can improve.

Even if my skin is black,
My heart is not dimmer,
Kindness is what you lack,
But there is still hope, just a glimmer.

Although I was sent to jail,
I know I did not fail.
I hope I helped people everywhere,
And made the world a bit more fair.

Ahad Usman (13)

Infinity

Always passing by
I am the healer of all
I will never die
Yet I appear small
A part of nature
That you will never see
Impossible to capture
You can only represent me
I have seen everything
From the past to the present
Constantly moving
I am something to be spent.

Tricia Currie

The Virus

C ough, cough, cough
O h no, everyone run away
R un, run, run - the virus is here to stay
O n top of ledges, door handles and fences
N HS are our country's best defences
A way with the virus, I just want to play
but not in a year, I want it today.

Oliver Coburn (13)

Too Late

Stop.
Wait.
Go.
Too late.
Gone.
Life is as easy to navigate as red, amber, green
I am your home, your life, your sanctuary
And now it is your choice, your decision, your move
and the seconds, days, years tick by
but the traffic lights are all on red.
Stop.
I am dying.
Wait.
What can you do?
Go.
Too late.
Gone.

Lilian Turner (16)

Priceless

Every day the air grows thicker,
I see my friends die quicker,
But I strive and go on,
I know they are wrong,
We as a kingdom are priceless.

People should respect us,
We never make a huge fuss,
We are peaceful and kind,
No bad thoughts come to mind,
We would never cause any harm.
We as beings are priceless.

Milla Shuttleworth (13)

Home Life

As the sunsets, the rain starts to fall,
Your house becomes a prison,
You suddenly feel trapped,
The walls close in,
You give up faith,
With nowhere to go,
But home,
There's always another day,
With your rainbow up,
All we have to say is,
Thank you.

Bronwyn Greenaway (11)

A Horse's Wish

I walk around my paddock all day
All I have to eat is some straw and hay
All I want is for someone to play
I get shifted from one place to the next
All I wish is that I could stay
I jump, I do tricks to get people to pay
But the one wish for me is to have someone to play.

Melanie Safe (17)

Death Row

Crime committed
In a red angry haze
Prison!
Grey, dark, depressed
Curled up in a ball
What did I do?
Thirty days
A ten by eight cell
Butterflies in my tummy
Guilt in my mind
One day
Metal cell as cold as my heart
Soon I will be gone.

Henry Burns (12)

Hold Tightly

Hold tightly
As I gasp for air I soon know it's over,
Taken away from Mother and Papa,
When I plea from the ashes,
I soon realise,
My hope has been lost,

I hold tightly but shortly I am absent,
As I drift away from this life,
All that remembers me are my pair of shoes.

Will Keeley

A Whale's Tale

I am a whale
I deserve a life
Humans, please before disposing
Think of my strife
Your actions could take me away
From my children and my wife
We should all love
So please do not hurt me
Please take note of the words above.

Katie McCabe (15)

The Truth

Lurking in the depths,
Watching them swim,
This is their last breath,
Before they meet death.

As quick as a bullet,
I soared upwards,
Into a trap,
Made by *them*.

Is this the end,
Of the king of the seas?
All thanks to the
Humans with no teeth.

Aragan Sureskumar (14)

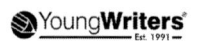

Rainbow

A haiku

We hold up rainbows,
to thank all the key workers,
they are amazing!

Isla Ennis-Smillie

YoungWriters

YOUNG WRITERS INFORMATION

We hope you have enjoyed reading this book – and that you will continue to in the coming years.

If you're a young writer who enjoys reading and creative writing, or the parent of an enthusiastic poet or story writer, do visit our website **www.youngwriters.co.uk**. Here you will find free competitions, workshops and games, as well as recommended reads, a poetry glossary and our blog. There's lots to keep budding writers motivated to write!

If you would like to order further copies of this book, or any of our other titles, then please give us a call or order via your online account.

Young Writers
Remus House
Coltsfoot Drive
Peterborough
PE2 9BF
(01733) 890066
info@youngwriters.co.uk

Join in the conversation!
Tips, news, giveaways and much more!

YoungWritersUK   @YoungWritersCW